# GEORGIA O'KEEFFE

J 2.3

KEEFFE, GEORGIA

# GEORGIA O'KEEFFE

## By Lloyd Goodrich
## and Doris Bry

Published for the
Whitney Museum of American Art
by Praeger Publishers

NEW YORK · WASHINGTON · LONDON

759.13
O

ENDPAPER: Sky Above Clouds IV. 1965. Oil on canvas. 8 × 24 feet.
FRONTISPIECE: Georgia O'Keeffe, 1951. Photograph by Doris Bry

Published in the United States of America in 1970
by Praeger Publishers, Inc.
111 Fourth Avenue, New York, N.Y. 10003
5 Cromwell Place, London S.W. 7, England
Library of Congress Catalogue Card Number: 72–129108
All rights reserved
Printed in the United States of America

# Foreword

THIS MONOGRAPH is published on the occasion of the retrospective exhibition of Georgia O'Keeffe's works organized by the Whitney Museum of American Art in 1970 and shown subsequently at the Art Institute of Chicago and the San Francisco Museum of Art.

The Whitney Museum wishes to express its deep indebtedness to Miss O'Keeffe for her cooperation in making her paintings, watercolors and drawings available for study, and for her generosity in lending many of them to the retrospective exhibition. For the writer it was a great pleasure to talk with her about her work and her life, and to have the privilege of visiting her in her New Mexico home, where she has created many of her finest paintings.

The Museum and the writer wish to record their gratitude to Doris Bry, friend and representative of Miss O'Keeffe, and authority on her work. As Guest Curator for the exhibition, Miss Bry was active in all phases of its selection and organization. As co-author of this monograph, she contributed the Chronology, the list of Principal Exhibitions, the Selected Bibliography, and the Catalogue; and she has supervised its production from first to last. She was of great assistance in furnishing information to the writer for his essay on the artist. In every aspect of the exhibition and publication, her knowledge and her devoted work have been invaluable.

In the middle 1940's the American Art Research Council, established by the Whitney Museum with the writer as Director and Rosalind Irvine as Secretary, undertook research on certain leading American artists. With Miss O'Keeffe's full cooperation, Miss Irvine assembled the most complete record of the artist's works up to that time. This record, continued by Miss Bry, was of great help in selecting the exhibition and preparing this monograph.

The Museum is grateful to Susan and David Workman for their interest in Miss O'Keeffe's art and their generous contribution toward the cost of research on it.

The plates in this monograph result from extensive experimentation and proofing with several printing processes. In this work Miss Bry was given the benefit of the special skills and constant interest of Harold Hugo, John Peckham, and James Barnett of The Meriden Gravure Company, Bert Clarke of Clarke & Way Inc., and Harry Baker of Publicity Engravers Inc. The cooperation of the Metropolitan Museum of Art, the Art Institute of Chicago, and private lenders in making their paintings available for color plate photography and proofing was greatly appreciated. The care given by Mrs. Caroline K. Keck and Felrath Hines as conservators for Miss O'Keeffe's paintings is gratefully acknowledged. James J. Lebron's meticulous supervision of the packing and transportation of the paintings was of the greatest assistance.

The writer wishes to thank Katharine Kuh for her kind permission to quote from her interview with Miss O'Keeffe included in her book *The Artist's Voice*, published by Harper & Row, New York, in 1962.

The Whitney Museum wishes to thank the following museums and collectors whose generosity in lending works made the retrospective exhibition possible:

Albright-Knox Art Gallery, Buffalo, New York; Amon Carter Museum of Western Art, Fort Worth, Texas; The Art Institute of Chicago; The Brooklyn Museum; City Art Museum of St. Louis; The Cleveland Museum of Art; The Currier Gallery of Art, Manchester, New Hampshire; Fisk University, Carl Van Vechten Gallery of Art, Nashville, Tennessee; The Metropolitan Museum of Art, New York; The Museum of Modern Art, New York; National Gallery of Art, Washington, D.C.; New Britain Museum of American Art, New Britain, Connecticut; The Phillips Collection, Washington, D.C.; Santa Barbara Museum of Art, California; Vassar College Art Gallery, Poughkeepsie, New York.

Lawrence H. Bloedel; Dr. Helen W. Boigon; The Bradley Family Foundation, Inc.; Mr. and Mrs. Charles E. Claggett; Dr. and Mrs. Milton M. Gardner; Jackie and Ulf Greber; Inland Steel Company; Mrs. Everett H. Jones; Mrs. Helen DeVitt Jones; William H. Lane Foundation; Wright Ludington; Mr. and Mrs. Stanley Marcus; Mr. and Mrs. Eugene McDermott; Miss Mary McDermott; Sidney and George Perutz; Daniel Catton Rich; Mrs. Frank Sebring; Mrs. Charles D. Tandy; Mr. and Mrs. Norton S. Walbridge; Mr. and Mrs. J. Carrington Woolley; Susan and David Workman; Mrs. Frank Lloyd Wright; Mrs. Robert R. Young.
                                                                                    L. G.

# Georgia O'Keeffe

## by Lloyd Goodrich

GEORGIA O'KEEFFE is a unique figure in contemporary American art. Her art is an individual one, expressing personal emotions and perceptions in a style that combines strength and crystalline clarity. The sources of her imagery lie in the world of nature, but nature interpreted with great freedom, from precise realism to abstraction as pure as music. Over fifty years ago she was a pioneer of native modern art, and throughout her long creative career she has continued to make some of the most original contributions to the art of our time.

She was born in 1887 in Sun Prairie, a small farming community in Wisconsin. Her father was of Irish descent; her mother, Hungarian and Dutch. She was the second child of seven. When she was about fifteen the family moved to Williamsburg, Virginia, where, she later recalled, "I lived in an old-fashioned house—open fires and a lot of brothers and sisters—and horses and trees."

She had started to draw early, and at ten had already made up her mind to be an artist. In 1905, not quite eighteen, she entered the Art Institute of Chicago, where her chief teacher was John Vanderpoel, draftsman and anatomist. After a winter in Chicago she returned home. In the fall of 1907 (about to be twenty) she enrolled in the Art Students League of New York.

The American art world of 1907 was completely conservative. The revolutionary modern movements abroad were still unknown here. In Paris some young Americans were coming in contact with modern art, but they had not yet returned. Alfred Stieglitz had started his innovating gallery at 291 Fifth Avenue, but his first show of an advanced painter—Matisse—was not to come until April 1908. For the art student of those days America had little to offer except slick academicism.

The dominating figure at the League was William M. Chase, who came to his class wearing a silk hat, spats and gloves, and who taught the brilliant brushwork of the Munich school—Frans Hals Americanized. O'Keeffe was an able pupil, and won a prize for a still life of a dead rabbit and a copper pot. But she was more clearheaded than her fellow students, and more of a rebel. "I began to realize," she recently told Katharine Kuh, "that a lot of people had done this same kind of painting before I came along. It had been done and I didn't think I could do it any better. It would have been just futile for me, so I stopped painting for quite a while." After a year at the League she returned to Virginia, destroyed her student work, and decided to give up painting. That she could see no alternative is a commentary on the state of American art education.

Instead, since she had to make a living, she took up commercial art, and spent a year in Chicago drawing lace and embroidery for advertisements. But this also seemed a dead end, and once again she returned home. The family moved to Charlottesville, site of the University of Virginia. Although she had stopped painting, in 1912 one of her sisters persuaded her to visit a summer art class at the University, and she became so interested that she enrolled in it. The teacher was Alon Bement, a disciple of Arthur Wesley Dow, head of the fine arts department of Teachers College, Columbia University. Dow was one of the few sophisticated American art educators of the time. He had spent years abroad, had been with Gauguin at Pont Aven, and through the Orientalist Ernest Fenollosa had become an ardent admirer of Japanese and Chinese art. As a teacher of teachers he rejected realism and based his system on the principles of design as he interpreted them in Far Eastern art: flat patterning, simplification, harmony. It was a limited aesthetic, but compared to academicism, an oasis in the desert. "It was Arthur Dow who affected my start," O'Keeffe has said, "who helped me to find something of my own. . . . This man had one dominating idea: to fill a space in a beautiful way."

So she decided to become a teacher. After two weeks in Bement's class he invited her to teach at the University the following summer. But first she had to have teaching experience. That fall she took a position as supervisor of art in the public schools of Amarillo in northwest Texas; and here she worked for two winters, returning in the summers to teach at the University of Virginia. Bement urged her to go to New York to study directly with Dow, which she did in 1914/15 and again in the spring of 1916. Then for two more years she taught at West Texas State Normal School, in Canyon, near Amarillo.

8

To most artists four winters in the Texas Panhandle would have seemed like exile to Siberia. But to O'Keeffe, used only to the green Midwest and South, this first encounter with the Southwest was a revelation. "I lived on the plains of North Texas for four years," she wrote in 1919. "It is the only place I have ever felt that I really belonged—that I really felt at home." It was a country of vast arid plains and wide skies, windswept, freezing in winter, without green grass or a tree of any size—so dry that there were no flowers for her pupils to paint. "But I belonged," O'Keeffe told a friend. "That was my country—terrible winds and a wonderful emptiness."

Her active teaching career in these years left little time for painting, but she managed to do some. In the fall of 1915, teaching for a semester at a small college in South Carolina, she found more time. One day she placed all her pictures around her room, locked the door, and studied them. She saw that every work showed the influence of someone else. "I realized that I had a lot of things in my head that others didn't have," she has said. "I made up my mind to put down what was in my head."

"I grew up pretty much as everybody else grows up," she wrote of this experience, in the catalogue of a one-man show in January 1923, "and one day seven years ago found myself saying to myself—I can't live where I want to—I can't go where I want to—I can't do what I want to—I can't even say what I want to—. School and things that painters have taught me even keep me from painting as I want to. I decided I was a very stupid fool not to at least paint as I wanted to and say what I wanted to when I painted as that seemed to be the only thing I could do that didn't concern anybody but myself—that was nobody's business but my own. —So these paintings and drawings happened and many others that are not here. —I found that I could say things with color and shapes that I couldn't say in any other way—things that I had no words for."

From that moment of self-revelation her creative career began. Its first fruits were a series of large charcoal drawings begun that fall. They were not the usual kind of drawings—studies from nature—but adventures in pictorial form and space. In some, a trace of Dow's example could be detected, in the compositional sense, the clearly defined outlines, the balance of lights and darks. But they were far from the neat Japanesque patterns of most of Dow's pupils. A vital creative energy was expressing itself in original terms.

Almost all of these drawings are abstract. Their forms suggest those of nature, but without specific imagery. They are marked by a quality not stressed by Dow: a sense of movement—not representation of moving things, but movement in the forms themselves. In *Drawing No. 13* the three separate elements—the undulating rising form, the succession of swelling bud-like shapes, and the series of acute angles—move in differing yet related tempos and in contrapuntal style. These three movements evoke natural forces: the soaring of flames, the reach of plants toward the light. Another kind of rhythm activates *Drawing No. 8*; revolving spirals closing in on a center of relative stillness, like the eye of a hurricane. In *Drawing No. 12* the motif is again curvilinear motion: a dominant upward thrust leading to an inward-turning spiral. On the other hand, a few drawings have realistic subjects: *Drawing No. 15*, for example, pictures the rolling contours of a Texas canyon, embodied in a few broad rhythmic forms.

At the same time O'Keeffe began to express her new concepts in watercolors. Some of them were representational, mostly landscapes: plains and sky, at sunrise and sunset, in moonlight and starlight. One series of three was titled *Light Coming on the Plains*. Others were entirely abstract, their titles just the main colors, such as *Red and Green*. All these watercolors were very broad and free, with simple forms and strong, sometimes violent color—direct emotional expression, of explosive force. She was letting herself go in them even more than in her drawings, which were more consciously designed. As with the drawings, one has the feeling that these were private documents.

In December 1915 O'Keeffe sent a group of her new drawings to a friend and fellow student at Teachers College, Anita Pollitzer; they had been writing each other frequently, and the drawings were a form of letter. With them came a strict injunction not to show them to anyone. Miss Pollitzer had often visited Alfred Stieglitz's gallery, 291. Disregarding her friend's admonition, she took the drawings to Stieglitz, who examined them and said, "Finally a woman on paper." He studied and discussed them with his fellow artists, and in May included them in an exhibition with works by two other painters. O'Keeffe, now back at Columbia, heard of this, descended on 291 and demanded that they be taken down.

10

But Stieglitz won the argument, and they remained. Thus began an association, professional and personal, that was to last the rest of Stieglitz's life.

A pioneer artist-photographer, and one of the greatest, Stieglitz was a magnetic personality, attracting devoted friends and admirers. He had made 291 a center of advanced art, and had been the first to show many European modernists in this country. But he also believed strongly in the future of American art, and particularly in certain younger artists whom he took under his wing, and for whom he made it possible to work without too many financial worries.

In April 1917, a year after showing her drawings, Stieglitz gave O'Keeffe her first one-man exhibition, of drawings and watercolors. It was also the last show at 291; the building was about to be torn down, and Stieglitz was temporarily wearied by arranging exhibitions. O'Keeffe was teaching in Texas, but she came East to see the gallery for the last time. The exhibition had been taken down, but Stieglitz rehung it for her to see. It was then that he took the first of the many photographs of her which were among his finest works. The following spring she came again to New York at the suggestion of Stieglitz, who offered her a year in which to paint—something she had been unable to do except for short periods. At the end of the summer she resigned from her Texas job and remained in the East, free at last from teaching.

"When '291' ended in 1917," Doris Bry has written, "Stieglitz was free, for the first time since 1905, to photograph without the strain of constant exhibitions. . . . No intelligent consideration of his later photographs can be made without mention of his relationship to O'Keeffe, for this remained the center of his life and work until his death in 1946. . . .

"After '291' came to an end, the first series in which Stieglitz became absorbed was the portrait of Georgia O'Keeffe. Starting in 1917 and continuing until he put down his heavy cameras in 1937, the O'Keeffe portrait as he left it consists of prints from about 500 negatives. Ideally, Stieglitz believed that a photographic portrait should begin with birth, continue throughout life until death, and then continue with the subject's child. To show the many facets of a person, the true portrait had to be many prints which, seen together, would convey more than the same photographs seen one at a time. Hands, feet, torsos, tones and lines, molded by every possible experience, mood, and emotion—taken over the years—all belonged. His concept was challenging and impossible, but he came nearer to achieving it in his photographs of O'Keeffe than in any other group of his prints. Although the Stieglitz portrait of O'Keeffe inevitably has its roots in the photographer and his subject, the series of prints transcends the two individuals concerned and becomes a moving symbol of the range of possibilities, life, and beauty inherent in human relationships."

For eight years Stieglitz had no gallery of his own, but he organized exhibitions of his artists in other galleries, including two O'Keeffe shows at the Anderson Galleries, in 1923 and 1924. Then in 1925 he opened The Intimate Gallery which continued until 1930, when he started An American Place, which he ran until his death. In these two galleries he held twenty annual exhibitions of O'Keeffe's new works. She was one of five American painters (the others being Demuth, Dove, Hartley, and Marin) on whom he concentrated. He always retained his gift for attracting advanced creative individuals, and he and O'Keeffe had a wide circle of friends in all the arts. Few painters have had a more universally favorable press than she had from the very first; and the reviews of her exhibitions, which Stieglitz often reprinted in his catalogues, form a unique record of admiration by the leading art writers of the time, and by fellow artists. That her head was not turned by them is a tribute to her fundamental commonsense, and in the case of the more fervid, to her sense of humor.

At the same time that she was producing her first original drawings and watercolors, in 1915, O'Keeffe was also working in oils. At first her paintings were small and rather tentative, like her watercolors in their broad, summary forms, emphatic rhythms and primary colors. Passionate feeling was expressing itself violently, sometimes crudely. But with the summer of 1918, when she had her first free time to paint, her style gained greatly in maturity. The paintings of that year and 1919 were the first in which she realized herself fully in the heavier medium. Most of them were abstract, without recognizable imagery. But judging by the character of the forms, and the titles of the few that were not simply given numbers, the primary sources were in nature, and particularly the Southwest. *From the Plains*, with its dark earth forms against the sky, is alive with a sense of light, space and wind. In *Orange and Red Streak* the brilliant arc shooting across the dark background suggests the drama of light prevailing over darkness, as in the 1917 watercolors, *Light Coming on the Plains*. But others cannot be related to anything specific in nature. *Blue and Green Music* is pure movement and energy: straight lines thrusting diagonally downward, countered by rising flame-like shapes. Such paintings were no longer tentative, but absolutely sure.

The style of abstraction that O'Keeffe had evolved was purely personal, an intense subjective expression, with no discernible influences from without. And the forms it created were entirely individual. Differing from the more or less flat patterns of geometric abstraction, her forms exist in space; they are three-dimensional. Unlike cubism's basis in actual objects and figures, the substance of her forms bears no resemblance to anything concrete; it has neither texture nor tactile qualities. Its nearest equivalent in the "real" world is light—colored light. Even in its closest approach to solid substance, as in the *Black Spot* series, it is simply colored forms, with no identifiable relation to actuality. This disembodiment gives her abstractions a visionary quality. They have close analogies to music; they are a kind of visual music. Indeed, several of her titles refer to music: *Blue and Green Music* and *Music, Pink and Blue*. As with music, one of their essential elements is rhythmic movement.

Unlike most other American modernists, O'Keeffe's work of the time showed little relation to international abstract art. Cubism was concerned with the forms and physical properties of figures and objects, and their reconstruction in plastic terms, without expression of subjective emotion. By contrast, O'Keeffe's art was charged with personal emotion. Nor did she have anything in common with geometric abstraction like that of the Dutch de Stijl school, with their concept of a painting as a two-dimensional physical object, their avoidance of sensations of round forms and deep space. Her creation of projection and recession by the play of warm and cool colors suggests parallels with Orphism and its American rival Synchromism, but with her this ability was not the result of theory but of instinct; and in any case the content of her art was different. Perhaps the closest parallel was the contemporary style of Kandinsky, with his emotional expressionism and conscious relation to music, but there is no evidence of any influence such as that of Kandinsky on Marsden Hartley. O'Keeffe's early abstractions were among the most original manifestations of native modernism in America.

13

The unearthliness of her abstract imagery was carried further in the two paintings called *Music, Pink and Blue*—conceptions with little relation to the actual world, yet hauntingly real. Highly-colored diaphanous folds surround a deep blue opening which might be the sky. (It is interesting to compare this with the pelvis paintings of twenty-five years later.) Again, the substance is immaterial, the image visionary; but the color has become startling. This trend was continued with *Grey Line with Black, Blue and Yellow*, into a chromatic range that seems to include all the hues of the spectrum. The many-colored folds surround a dark cavity, whose mysterious depths are in dramatic contrast with the luminous folds around it. The image has sexual overtones, but sublimated into an imaginative pictorial creation, in colors pushed to maximum intensity—on the verge of gaudiness, but overpowering in their boldness. In this and similar works O'Keeffe was demonstrating that she had absolutely no inhibitions about color. Sometimes her works of this kind recall the way-out fantasies seen in the Independent Society shows of the time; but actually they were far from naive. She was simply being absolutely herself, as always. Her color with its prismatic brilliancy and its complete freedom from canons of good taste was prophetic of present-day color painting, with the considerable difference that her color was not used in flat patterns or overall unmodulated color fields, but to create three-dimensional forms and space.

This chromatic phase was by no means the only one in O'Keeffe's abstract art of the 1920's. One of her characteristics is that (except when she is working deliberately in a series) each picture is an individual creation. Nothing could be less like *Grey Line with Black, Blue and Yellow* than *Abstraction* of three years later: limited in color, almost a monochrome, with the whole emphasis on the crystal-clear forms, the play of interweaving lines, the mysterious vertical cleft in the immaculate surface. *Black Abstraction* of 1927 and *Black and White* of 1930 are just what their titles indicate. In both, the absence of other colors adds to their power; they are simplified, concentrated statements of the utmost force. It is noteworthy that these black and white works, and others, antedate by a good many years the abstract expressionists' black paintings.

A marked feature of O'Keeffe's art has always been the variety of her artistic language. At one and the same time she has practised abstraction and representation, and many variations between them. At the opposite pole from her abstract works are those in which objects and places are portrayed with precise realism. In between come all degrees of free representation and semi-abstraction. Sometimes her style is selective realism. Sometimes the motif is pictured realistically but in unreal, imaginative contexts: magnified far beyond its actual dimensions, removed from its normal setting, shown in strange combinations. Sometimes the motif serves as a starting point for plastic invention, and is so altered as to become semi-abstract. And sometimes her work is purely abstract, with little or no relation to specific actualities.

But even at her most realistic, she is concerned not with the mere visual appearance of things, but with their essential life, their being, their identity. The thing-in-itself is what matters. Photographic illusionism is disregarded in favor of basic form. The object is re-created in plastic terms. The forms of nature are translated into the forms of art. Hence her naturalistic works have a formal quality that can be called abstract, just as her abstract works usually have their origins in nature. There is no conflict between these two poles of her modes of expression; the same content and the same spirit are in both. She has never been bound by any rigid creed, but has always been free to speak in the language appropriate for the particular theme and mood.

All her work, whether abstract or representational, has the fundamental physical existence that is the basis of all vital art. Through pigment, color, line and form it speaks directly to the senses. It makes a frank statement, without timidity or evasion. But beneath even the most brilliant of her surfaces there are depths that reveal the basic three-dimensional structure. Without theorizing, she has an unerring awareness of the picture plane, the pictorial space beyond which forms cannot project or spaces recede without destroying the plastic unity of the work.

Absolute clarity marks her style; there is nothing vague about it. The element of mystery which does exist in some works is due not to obscurity but to their clear-cut but enigmatic images and forms. Her lucidity never becomes a mannerism; it is an innate characteristic of her personal vision. Edges are precise but not hard; they round the forms into depth. Her art has an essential refinement that involves no loss of strength; it is capable of both delicacy and power. There is often a degree of severity in her style. Everything is simplified to essentials; there are no unnecessary details. This simplification sometimes produces works of minimal forms and colors, but of maximum impact. Again there can be a profusion of elements, but always selective. Her art presents a rare combination of austerity and a deep sensuousness.

The world of nature is the primary source of most of her works. She has seldom pictured the human figure; she says, humorously, because "I have sat to so many artists that I would never ask anyone to do the same for me"; but the reasons lie deeper than that. To her, nature contains all that she needs for her art: sun and sky; mountains, plains and deserts; trees, flowers, plants, and all kinds of growing things; and common objects—stones, dead leaves, weathered wood, animals' bones—objects not generally regarded as things of beauty.

O'Keeffe's wide range of expression was evidenced early in her career. In 1919, when she was working mostly in abstract terms, she was also painting some representational pictures. With the beginning of the 1920's there were fewer abstractions, but she continued to produce them, and they were among her most original creations. But representational works began to predominate in numbers; and this remained true for the next two decades.

At first her most frequent subjects were flowers, still life, plants and landscape. These motifs came mostly from her summers at Lake George, New York, where Stieglitz occupied a farmhouse on his family's estate. Since the country has always meant more to her than the city, she usually went there in April and stayed late into the fall. Her Lake George landscapes, compared to the Southwest subjects, were inclined to be quiet and sometimes somber, pervaded by a sober Northern mood. Dark mountains against the sky; the lake seen at night, under stars; severe lines of farm buildings; black crows flying across the water at dusk; a chestnut tree silhouetted against a sunset sky, with a single star. Here was a kind of nature poetry that few modern artists of the time were attempting; who among the modernists would dare to paint a sunset? In these landscapes, as in all her works, she was paying no attention to current trends. The style was relatively naturalistic, but much simplified, with emphasis on the strong rhythmic lines of mountains, trees and clouds.

The most striking representational painting of a Lake George subject is *Farmhouse Window and Door*, originally called *Portrait of the Farmhouse*. Though entirely realistic, its severe simplification, stark rectangular forms and austere color harmony, and the fine relations of all elements, give it the quality of a handsome abstract design. It is interesting to compare Stieglitz's photograph of the same subject, taken at an angle and more complex in composition, with O'Keeffe's direct frontal, symmetrical design.

More individual than most of her naturalistic Lake George works were those in which nature provided themes for abstract or semi-abstract invention. In *From the Lake, No. 3* the motif is evidently things seen through water, like looking down at the bottom of a lake. There is no literal imagery; rather, a translation of the motif into shapes and colors that capture the sense of translucency, flow, shifting images, the spirit of water. The seemingly meandering lines are actually so directed as to produce a complex, rich linear design. One of O'Keeffe's special gifts is this ability to create, out of nature's inexhaustible variety, works of art that are vital and alive, and at the same time clear and controlled.

One constant factor throughout O'Keeffe's career has been her love of the physical objects of nature. Concentrating on the object, she isolates it from the world of ordinary reality, and gives it a new significance. It was in 1924 that she began to paint the magnified flowers with which she is most commonly identified by the public. For several years previously she had been painting flowers, but they were normal in scale. Already, however, she was concentrating on the single flower—no bouquets in vases, like the usual lady flower painter.

"A flower is relatively small," she wrote in 1939. "Everyone has many associations with a flower—the idea of flowers. You put out your hand to touch the flower—lean forward to smell it—maybe touch it with your lips almost without thinking—or give it to someone to please them. Still—in a way—nobody sees a flower—really—it is so small—we haven't time—and to see takes time like to have a friend takes time. If I could paint the flower exactly as I see it no one would see what I see because I would paint it small like the flower is small.

17

"So I said to myself—I'll paint what I see—what the flower is to me but I'll paint it big and they will be surprised into taking time to look at it—I will make even busy New Yorkers take time to see what I see of flowers."

The sensuous beauty of flowers, their miracles of shapes, textures and colors, have seldom been given such intense expression in painting as in these magnified flower pictures. By enormously enlarging the flower she transformed it, gave it not only a new dimension but a new kind of existence. Magnification enabled her to reveal its structure with complete clarity. The flower became a world in itself, a microcosm. Magnification was another kind of abstraction, of separating the object from ordinary reality, and endowing it with a life of its own.

One noticeable feature of the flower paintings is their frontal presentation. The flower faces us directly, wide open. It is thus seen in its most effective position, in which its forms and colors can be realized most fully—just as we can see and understand another person most clearly if he is facing us and not turned away. This frontal presentation had appeared in some of her earliest works, such as *Grey Line with Black, Blue and Yellow*; and it continued in paintings that featured the individual physical object: among others, *Farmhouse Window and Door*, *Black Cross, New Mexico*, and her later paintings of animals' skulls.

In the flower paintings nature's organisms often bore sexual associations. The forms were flower forms, but they also suggested the forms of the body, its subtle lines, its curves and folds and hidden depths; and the colors and textures recalled the fineness and bloom and delicate colors of flesh. This ambivalence of imagery, which is characteristic of O'Keeffe and part of the depth and power of her art, this sexual magnetism beneath the visible forms, added to the spell and mystery of her flower paintings, and made them among her most sensitive and living creations. This sense of sex—one of the motivating forces in all vital art, even when highly sublimated—was in harmony with her feeling for the life in nature, for growth in flower and plant, for the movement of all living things toward light and heat.

When her flower paintings were first exhibited, Freudianism (and pseudo-Freudianism) was very much in the air. The critics wrote extensively if somewhat evasively about this aspect of her art. Some of this was perceptive, some hyperbolic. All of it disturbed O'Keeffe, and still does. As she wrote in 1939, in the statement already quoted: "Well—I made you take time to look at what I saw and when you took time to really notice my flower you hung all your own associations with flowers on my flower and you write about my flower as if I think and see what you think and see of the flower—and I don't."

From early in her career O'Keeffe has often created in series: four, five, six or more pictures based on a single theme. This method began with her 1915 watercolors, and it has continued ever since. Usually she begins with a motif in nature, and in successive paintings transforms it from the more or less naturalistic to the abstract or semi-abstract. As she has said: "I work on an idea for a long time. It's like getting acquainted with a person, and I don't get acquainted easily." And again: "Sometimes I start in very realistic fashion, and as I go on from one painting to another of the same thing, it becomes simplified till it can be nothing but abstract."

One such sequence was the *Shell and Old Shingle* series of 1926, whose starting point was a weathered shingle and a clam shell, and which went through seven stages of increasingly abstracted designs in subtle grays and off-whites, painted with a delicate skill and a sensuous feeling for pigment that remind us that she had won a still life prize in Chase's class—but this is closer to Manet. The last of the series, strangely, is a landscape of Lake George, which (she realized after finishing it) continued the shape and color of the shingle. These series paintings are never merely repetitions; each work presents a new concept.

A completely different note is sounded in the *Jack-in-the-Pulpit* series of 1930: large in scale, bold in style, in a color scheme of deep grayed purple and strong greens. The six paintings begin with a small relatively naturalistic portrayal of the plant. Number 2 displays a giant plant, presented with almost posterlike impact. Number 3 is simplified and more deliberately designed, with a gain in massiveness and strength. Number 4 marks a radical change: the flower alone, enormously magnified. Then Number 5, the largest of the series, expands into an abstract design that is completely new, yet retains the character of shapes and colors of its predecessors. Its powerful forms rise from the ground, thrust upward, and culminate in a triumphant swirling flourish. After this one might wonder what more could be said on the theme; but Number 6 presents just the pistil of the flower, dark against a white radiance like a halo. The form grows in strength as it rises, and its color changes from gray to an intense purplish black at the head. The style is of the utmost simplicity. This black shape with its white halo has a visionary presence.


In the mid-1920's O'Keeffe and Stieglitz lived in the Shelton Hotel in mid-town New York, on the thirtieth floor, with a spectacular view of the East River and neighboring skyscrapers. Here she painted about fifteen city scenes, between 1926 and 1929. They were quite unlike anything she had done before in subject matter, and to some extent in style. The majority were paintings of particular skyscrapers; the viewpoint was often from high up, and the emphasis was on perpendicularity. Many were night scenes: tall buildings looming up like dark monoliths, or presenting patterns of lighted windows and illuminated ornate tops. There was a romantic feeling for the visual excitement of the city at night: street lights, clouds lighted by the city's glow, sometimes a glimpse of the moon, sky signs (one of them reads "ALFRED STIEGLITZ"). Another touch of fantasy was *The Shelton with Sunspots*: a sunburst echoed by sunspots all over the picture, like the after-image one gets from looking at the sun. More factual were several pictures of the East River as seen from her window; almost identical views, differing chiefly in scale and details. These were among her most realistic works, with the individual buildings, factories and power plants precisely rendered.

These city subjects naturally called for a geometric style. Marked by her characteristic simplification, they created handsome patterns of straight lines and rectangular shapes. In these respects they were close to the trend of the time that has been called precisionism. But O'Keeffe was never a precisionist in the sense that Sheeler, Demuth, Spencer and others were. These men used the phenomena of urban and industrial America—factories, railroads, skyscrapers, machine-made products, and sometimes the machine itself—to create formal designs marked by exactness, hard edges and geometric forms. But with O'Keeffe such subjects and such a style have made up only a very small minority of her works. She has no love of the machine and its products. Aside from her relatively few city scenes, her most precisionist works have been of country buildings—farmhouses and barns. While one of her characteristics is precision, the large majority of her paintings have no trace of geometric style.

In 1917 O'Keeffe had had her first glimpse of New Mexico on a trip to Colorado. But it was twelve years before she saw the state again, in 1929, when she spent a summer in Taos. It was an experience that was to change the whole course of her life. The Texas plains had not prepared her for the extraordinary beauty of the desert country. Every new sight entranced her: as her friend Mabel Dodge Luhan reported: " 'Wonderful' was a word that was always on her lips. . . . 'No one told me it was like *this.*' "

Thereafter she spent almost every summer in New Mexico, the rest of the year with Stieglitz in the East. But though the artistic and literary community of Taos welcomed her, it was not there that she finally settled, but seventy miles west. Near the village of Abiquiu she found an adobe house in the Ghost Ranch, a wild area far in from any road, facing south toward the Pedernal, an old volcanic peak with a flat top, and north toward a range of high sheer rock cliffs. For several summers she rented the house, then bought it in 1940. After Stieglitz's death in 1946, and the three years she devoted to the complicated affairs of his estate, she left New York for good and settled year-round in New Mexico.

The Ranch had always been too remote for winter living; so in 1945 she bought a second house in the village of Abiquiu, and here she has spent the winters, with summers in the ranch house. Abiquiu, on top of a hill, is a small long-settled community of Americans of Spanish and Indian descent; and she is one of the very few persons in it who are not Spanish-American. The one-story adobe house was almost a ruin; the roof had fallen in, and the house was being used as a pigpen. But she got local men and women to rebuild it (the women are the best adobe masons). The old house surrounds a patio; across a courtyard are the former stables, now her studio and living quarters, commanding a magnificent view across the Chama River valley toward many-colored mesas and hills. The establishment is almost completely self-sufficient. Fruit trees and a large garden provide all the vegetables and fruit. Wheat is ground by hand for the home-baked bread. In cold weather, gas heating is supplemented by pungent-smelling piñon fires in every room. With the help of a man-of-all-work she packs all her paintings for shipment. She loves music, and her record collection and player are the best. When she says, "This is the place for me," there is no doubt about it.

The surrounding country is not the Grand Canyon with its monumental spectacularity, but the beautiful desert country. Mountains, mesas and hills, carved by millennia of erosion into fantastic forms of endless variety—cliffs, rock chimneys, precipices, gulleys, dry waterfalls—extend as far as the eye can see. They are of every imaginable color: red, black, yellow, purple, gold, lavender, and many delicate colored grays. Their bare slopes are dotted with green clumps of juniper and piñon. When a cloud passes over the sun, the colors change in a hundred ways. The green valley of the red Chama is lined with silvery cottonwood trees. Abiquiu is six thousand feet above sea level, and the air is crystal clear, the sky is very deep blue, and at night the stars seem within reach.

A few times O'Keeffe has said in written words what she feels about this country. In the catalogue of her 1939 exhibition she wrote: "A flower touches almost everyone's heart. A red hill doesn't touch everyone's heart as it touches mine and I suppose there is no reason why it should. The red hill is a piece of the bad lands where even the grass is gone. Bad lands roll away outside my door — hill after hill—red hills of apparently the same sort of earth that you mix with oil to make paint. All the earth colors of the painter's palette are out there in the many miles of bad lands. The light Naples yellow through the ochres—orange and red and purple earth—even the soft earth greens. You have no associations with those hills—our waste land—I think our most beautiful country."

She never tires of painting it. The Southwest has been painted often—but often badly, by artists who believe that a beautiful subject produces a beautiful picture. But O'Keeffe translates this landscape into the language of art. She models the hills so that they possess substance and weight. She carves their intricate folded and furrowed forms into powerful sculptural creations. The unbelievable colors of the desert are recorded, without sweetening, in full-bodied earthy harmonies. Always her desert poetry is embodied in robust physical language, speaking to the senses.

Her first summer in New Mexico resulted in many paintings that were new not only in subjects but in the vitality of their style. In *Black Cross, New Mexico*,

22

the overwhelming powerful form of the cross fills the canvas and seems to burst out of its limits. It is silhouetted against miles of bare hills and a serene evening sky with a single star and a streak of blood-red sunset—an unforgettable image that sums up the somber tragic spirit of Spanish Catholicism in this land of the Penitentes.

Frequently her paintings of the desert country have passed over from representation to abstraction. The original motif of the *Black Place* series of 1944 was a remarkable formation of black earth with a deep vertical cleft down its center. In the three *Black Place* paintings the cleft has been transformed into a black shape like a great arrow, plunging down into lower depths. Five years later, in the abstract *Black Place Green*, the arrow has become a spearhead, whose dominating form creates one of her most powerful designs.

Since she first came to New Mexico her love of the physical objects of nature has been centered on things that are part of the desert country. Her Abiquiu house contains a collection of hundreds of stones of all sizes, shapes, colors and surfaces, picked up by her in the desert, plus some sent by distant friends. They have been the subjects of numerous paintings. In both houses (especially the Ranch) are many animals' bones from the desert: skulls, horns, vertebrae and pelvises of deer, antelopes, cows, rams, horses and mules—worn by wind and water to fine, fragile, shell-like textures, and bleached by the sun to pallid, delicate whites and grays.

Before she had settled permanently in New Mexico she wrote, in 1939: "I have wanted to paint the desert and I haven't known how. I always think that I can not stay with it long enough. So I brought home the bleached bones as my symbols of the desert. To me they are as beautiful as anything I know. To me they are strangely more living than the animals walking around—hair, eyes and all with their tails switching. The bones seem to cut sharply to the center of something that is keenly alive on the desert even tho' it is vast and empty and untouchable—and knows no kindness with all its beauty."

In 1931 she began to paint the bones—at first, animals' skulls with horns and antlers. They were painted realistically, with a precision and refinement equal to her flower paintings. Occasionally they were shown as a kind of still life, in ordi-

23

nary settings. But then she would place a flower on a skull—a startling juxtaposition of seeming opposites, the dead and the living, but to her evidently not opposed.

Then the presentation becomes more complex and further from the everyday world. The skull is removed from any realistic setting, isolated, suspended in space. In *Cow's Skull, Red, White and Blue* the white skull, unsupported, is presented frontally against a red, blue and black background, like an emblem on a banner. The horns and the vertical black band form a cross, reminiscent of *Black Cross, New Mexico*. The upper half of the skull, like the background, is painted flatly, but the lower half is broken up into jagged fragmented forms—one of her most accomplished passages of painting. The picture is a stunning combination of the flat and the modelled—a *tour de force*, of maximum boldness and impact.

Later, in works such as *From the Faraway Nearby*, the skull appears outdoors, floating above the desert—an apparition, yet completely tangible. In *Summer Days* the deer's skull and antlers with the accompanying handful of flowers exist in space, against empty sky and distant red hills. Each of the individual elements is painted with precise, exquisite realism, but their relations to one another have little to do with ordinary reality. The imagery in this and similar works is enigmatic; it might symbolize nature's eternal cycle of life and death, of mortality and new life, recurring endlessly in the space and light and impersonal beauty of the desert. These skull paintings continue the visionary strain of her earliest works, but in a far different language.

The bone pictures have sometimes been connected with surrealism. O'Keeffe denies any such connection, saying "I was in the surrealist show when I'd never heard of surrealism." Actually the surrealist movement, though launched in Paris in 1924, did not become acclimated in America until the late 1930's and early 1940's, when several of its European leaders arrived in this country. Before then, O'Keeffe had been one of the first native exponents of free imagery, all of whom were individual figures, unconnected with the organized, highly articulate European movement. In any case, her art differed fundamentally from surrealism. It had no relation to psychoanalysis, no conscious use of the subconscious, no deliberate irrationality. Its imagery was simpler, and closer to the world of nature. And she showed none of the surrealists' desire to *épater le bourgeois*.

24

In 1943 began a new series of bone pictures—the pelvis paintings. When they were first exhibited the following year (in the midst of World War II), she wrote a statement, "About Painting Desert Bones":

"I have picked flowers where I found them—

"Have picked up sea shells and rocks and pieces of wood where there were sea shells and rocks and pieces of wood that I liked

"When I found the beautiful white bones on the desert I picked them up and took them home too

"I have used these things to say what is to me the wideness and wonder of the world as I live in it

"A pelvis bone has always been useful to any animal that has it—quite as useful as a head I suppose. For years in the country the pelvis bones lay about the house indoors and out—always underfoot—seen and not seen as such things can be—seen in many different ways. I do not remember picking up the first one but I remember from when I first noticed them always knowing I would one day be painting them. A particularly beautiful one that I found on the mountain where I went fishing this summer started me working on them

"I was the sort of child that ate around the raisin on the cookie and ate around the hole in the doughnut saving either the raisin or the hole for the last and best

"so probably—not having changed much—when I started painting the pelvis bones I was most interested in the holes in the bones—what I saw through them —particularly the blue from holding them up in the sun against the sky as one is apt to do when one seems to have more sky than earth in one's world—

"They were most wonderful against the Blue—that Blue that will always be there as it is now after all man's destruction is finished

"I have tried to paint the Bones and the Blue."

The first pelvis paintings show the bones floating, bleached white, against a blue sky which shows through the holes. The frontal presentation of the skull pictures has been changed to viewpoints from varying angles. This makes their anatomy less easy to read, but creates extraordinary ambiguous forms. Unlike the skulls, the pelvis shapes fill the entire canvas, and often only part of them are included, so that they become magnified details. There are no accessories: no flowers, no backgrounds except the sky—only the bones and the blue. Their forms are fantastic—irregular, asymmetrical, pierced with openings, appearing as fragile as torn paper, and yet enduring. In their strange way they are alive with movement; they appear to be not only floating but flying. And their forms themselves flow in complicated rhythms.

In the pelvis subjects of the following year, the image has been simplified and concentrated: the chief element has become the single hole in the bone, and the sky seen through it. Magnification has increased. The forms of the surrounding bone, stripped to essentials, are shaped with great sensitiveness and subtlety. In their linear refinement and purity of form they are like abstract sculpture. In color, the series began with simple white and blue, but as the images become less realistic, so does the color; toward the last, the bones are sometimes red and white, the sky yellow. Concentrating on pure form, O'Keeffe in these pelvis paintings achieved some of her finest creations.


In the past two decades O'Keeffe's work has shown an increasing tendency toward abstraction. She has continued to paint representational pictures, and even her most abstract paintings are related to realities (indeed, she says they are realistic and not abstract). But the concrete realistic style of such works as the skull paintings has been replaced by more transformation of the motif into abstract terms.

One such motif is the patio of her Abiquiu house, a square open to the sun, with adobe walls, doors, and tile steppingstones. The patio provided subjects for over twenty paintings, from 1946 to 1960. They are among her most austerely simplified works, dealing with only five elements—wall, door, steppingstones, ground and sky, shown in varying seasons and lights, and from different angles— painted in a few simple earth colors, finely related. One series is frontally presented, and almost geometric; the successive versions become increasingly abstract, until in the last, *White Patio with Red Door*, the door is a rectangle in an overall space, the steppingstones have become a line of small flat rectangles, and the color has been reduced to red and white. These patio paintings are continuous uncompromising experiments in the relations of a few simple forms and colors.

A noteworthy feature of O'Keeffe's art is the recurrence of certain images through the years. Concepts which meant much to her in the past are not forgotten, but re-created in different form. In 1919 she had painted *From the Plains*, of which she wrote in 1957: "It was painted from something I heard very often —a very special rhythm that would go on for hours and hours. That was why I painted it again a couple of years ago." In the second of these later versions, *From the Plains II*, a great arch of light curves up and across the picture; it is armed with sharp spearheads, of which the strong upper ones determine the dominant movement. At the lower right is a small shape like wind-driven clouds lit by the sun. The design is a fine balance between two dynamic elements, one large and overpowering, the other small and concentrated, but holding its own. The painting is filled with a sense of space and light and the play of natural forces. A concept preserved through the years has been enlarged, simplified and expressed with the greatest power.

Differing from most of her fellow artists, O'Keeffe in her youth had showed no desire to go abroad. Her first trip outside the United States was not until 1932, and then it was to the Gaspé country in Canada, where she painted the plain white barns, among her most geometric works, and also the poignant *Cross by the Sea*, so opposite in mood from *Black Cross, New Mexico*. In 1939 she spent three months in Hawaii, and in the 1950's she went to Mexico and Peru.

Her first visit to Europe did not come until her middle sixties, in 1953. She had said that if she did go, it would be to see the country rather than the art; but actually she enjoyed both. In Spain she was impressed by the bullfights as well as by the Prado; and two recent trips to Vienna were not so much to see the Kunsthistorisches Museum as the famous Lipizzan horses of the Spanish Riding School, whose performances she says are like music.

On the other hand, in recent years she has traveled widely in other parts of the world. In 1959 she went around the world for three and a half months, by air, with stopovers including seven weeks in India. She prefers the Orient to Europe, and the following year she visited the Far East again. Within the United States she has taken trips through the Western mountain and canyon country, and in 1961 she went down the Colorado River on a rubber raft. And every year she flies several times between New Mexico and New York.

This experience of air travel in recent years has opened up an entirely new field of subject matter. One series of paintings, from 1958 to 1960, originated in seeing the earth from the air, particularly the lines of rivers and streams meandering over the earth's surface. "I've been flying a lot recently," she told Katharine Kuh a few years ago, "and I noticed a surprising number of deserts and wonderful rivers. The rivers actually seem to come up and hit you in the eye. There's nothing abstract about those pictures; they are what I saw—and very realistic to me. I must say I changed the color to suit myself, but after all you can see any color you want when you look out the window. . . . You see such marvellous things, such incredible colors." In her paintings the ribbonlike lines of rivers, twisting tortuously, doubling up on themselves, are often similar in form, but the color can be completely different, with titles such as *It Was Blue and Green* and *It Was Yellow and Pink*—startling colors, as if seen through varicolored atmosphere. Here is the visionary world of the air traveler, so different from the pedestrian view below. Its dreamlike aura recalls her early abstractions.

Sky and clouds as seen from a plane have been the theme of other paintings. In *Sky above White Clouds I* the cloud bank is unbroken and the composition consists simply of two broad areas of color: the white cloud cover, and the sky with its bands of blue and yellow-green. More complex is the *Sky above Clouds* series: four paintings, three done in 1963, the fourth in 1965. In the first and smallest, the separate rounded clouds are relatively realistic and fluffy, like a flock of sheep. As the series progresses and the scale increases, the clouds become more individually shaped and precisely defined, and more numerous. The series culminates in *Sky above Clouds IV*—by far the largest canvas she has ever painted, twenty-four feet wide. It is an immense panorama of innumerable cloud shapes, forming a white assemblage through which one sees the deep blue atmosphere below them. As they recede toward the horizon they diminish in size but multiply in numbers, until they disappear over the curvature of the earth. Above is a clear blue and rose sky. In this major work O'Keeffe has achieved an overwhelming sense of great height and distance, and of serene, limitless space.

Nothing could be more different than her three most recent paintings; portraits of a black rock from her collection. The latest, *Black Rock with Blue, III,* is as absolutely of the earth as the cloud pictures are of the sky. It has all the power and purity of form of which she has long shown her mastery.

With all her wide range in content and artistic language, Georgia O'Keeffe's evolution has been marked by a fundamental consistency. She has been herself from the first. The transformations that have taken place in her art have come from within. Her subject matter has broadened, her artistry has grown steadily in strength and refinement, but the central character of her mind and her art have remained constant.

# Catalogue of the Exhibition

The arrangement which follows is chronological, with the exception of the first three works. All paintings are lent by Miss O'Keeffe, unless otherwise specified. Dimensions are in inches, with height preceding width. Works marked with an asterisk are illustrated.

*1. BLUE LINES. 1916.
Watercolor. 25 × 19.
The Metropolitan Museum of Art,
The Alfred Stieglitz Collection.

2. DRAWING NO. 9. 1915.
Charcoal. 25 × 19.

*3. DRAWING NO. 13. 1915.
Charcoal. 24¾ × 18⅞.
The Metropolitan Museum of Art,
The Alfred Stieglitz Collection.

4. DRAWING NO. 8. 1916.
Charcoal. 24¼ × 18¾.

*5. DRAWING NO. 15. 1916.
Charcoal. 19 × 24½.

6. BLUE NO. I. 1916.
Watercolor. 15¹¹⁄₁₆ × 11.
The Brooklyn Museum,
bequest of Mary T. Cockroft.

*7. BLUE NO. II. 1916.
Watercolor. 15⅞ × 11.
The Brooklyn Museum,
bequest of Mary T. Cockroft.

8. BLUE NO. III. 1916.
Watercolor. 15¹⁵⁄₁₆ × 11.
The Brooklyn Museum,
bequest of Mary T. Cockroft.

9. BLUE NO. IV. 1916.
Watercolor. 15¹⁵⁄₁₆ × 10¹⁵⁄₁₆.
The Brooklyn Museum,
bequest of Mary T. Cockroft.

10. MORNING SKY WITH HOUSES
AND WINDMILL. 1916.
Watercolor. 9 × 12.

11. PAINTING NO. 21. 1916.
Oil on board. 13⅜ × 16⅛.

*12. PAINTING NO. 22. 1916.
Oil on board. 12⅞ × 17¼.

13. DRAWING NO. 12. 1917.
Charcoal. 24 × 19.

14. CANYON WITH CROWS. 1917.
Watercolor. 9 × 12.

*15. EVENING STAR NO. IV. 1917.
Watercolor. 9 × 12.

16. EVENING STAR NO. V. 1917.
Watercolor. 9 × 12.
Mrs. Everett H. Jones.

17. EVENING STAR NO. VI. 1917.
Watercolor. 9 × 12.
Dr. and Mrs. Milton M. Gardner.

*18. LIGHT COMING ON THE PLAINS
NO. II. 1917. Watercolor. 12×9.
Amon Carter Museum of
Western Art, Fort Worth, Texas.

19. NUDE SERIES, VII. 1917.
Watercolor. 17¾×13⅜.

20. STARLIGHT NIGHT. 1917.
Watercolor. 9×12.

*21. ORANGE AND RED STREAK. 1919.
Oil on canvas. 27¼×23¼.

*22. BLACK SPOT NO. 3. 1919.
Oil on canvas. 24×16.

*23. BLUE AND GREEN MUSIC. 1919.
Oil on canvas. 23×19.
The Art Institute of Chicago,
The Alfred Stieglitz Collection.

*24. MUSIC—PINK AND BLUE NO. I.
1919. Oil on canvas. 35×29.

*25. 59TH STREET STUDIO. 1919.
Oil on canvas. 35×29.

*26. SERIES I, NO. 12. 1920.
Oil on canvas. 20×17.

*27. LAKE GEORGE WITH CROWS.
c. 1921. Oil on canvas. 28½×25.

28. ABSTRACTION OF STREAM. 1921.
Pastel. 27¾×17½.

29. LEAVES UNDER WATER. 1922.
Oil on canvas. 9×6.

30. SPRING. C.1922.
Oil on canvas. 36×30.
Vassar College Art Gallery,
bequest of Edna Bryner.

*31. GREY LINE WITH BLACK,
BLUE AND YELLOW. C.1923.
Oil on canvas. 48×30.

*32. DARK ABSTRACTION. 1924.
Oil on canvas. 24⅞×20⅞.
City Art Museum of St. Louis.

*33. FLOWER ABSTRACTION. 1924.
Oil on canvas. 48×30.

*34. FROM THE LAKE NO. 3. 1924.
Oil on canvas. 36×30.

35. PORTRAIT OF A DAY—THIRD
DAY. 1924.
Oil on canvas. 32×25.
Jackie and Ulf Greber.

*36. RED YELLOW AND BLACK
STREAK. 1924.
Oil on canvas. 39½×32.

37. BIRCH AND PINE TREE NO. I.
1925. Oil on canvas. 35×22.

*38. GREY TREE, LAKE GEORGE.
1925. Oil on canvas. 36×30.

*39. ABSTRACTION. 1926.
Oil on canvas. 30×18.
Whitney Museum of
American Art.

*40. BLACK IRIS. 1926.
Oil on canvas. 36×30.
The Metropolitan Museum of Art,
The Alfred Stieglitz Collection.

*41. CLOSED CLAM SHELL. 1926.
Oil on canvas. 20×9.
Private Collection.

*42. OPEN CLAM SHELL. 1926.
Oil on canvas. 20×9.
Private Collection.

43. SHELL AND OLD SHINGLE I. 1926.
Oil on canvas. 9×7.

*44. SHELL AND OLD SHINGLE II.
1926. Oil on canvas. 30×18.

45. SHELL AND OLD SHINGLE III.
1926. Oil on board. 10¾×6.

46. SHELL AND OLD SHINGLE IV.
1926. Oil on canvas. 9¾×7.

*47. SHELL AND OLD SHINGLE VI.
1926. Oil on canvas. 30×18.
Mr. and Mrs. Charles E. Claggett.

48. SHELL AND SHINGLE SERIES VII.
1926. Oil on canvas. 21×32.

*49. THE SHELTON WITH SUNSPOTS.
1926. Oil on canvas. 48⅝×30⅝.
Inland Steel Company.

*50. ABSTRACTION—WHITE ROSE II.
1927. Oil on canvas. 36×30.
Private Collection.

51. ABSTRACTION—WHITE ROSE III.
1927. Oil on canvas. 36×30.

*52. BLACK ABSTRACTION. 1927.
Oil on canvas. 30×40¼.
The Metropolitan Museum of Art,
The Alfred Stieglitz Collection.

53. MORNING GLORY WITH BLACK.
1926. Oil on canvas. 40×30.
The Cleveland Museum of Art,
bequest of Leonard C. Hanna, Jr.

*54. RADIATOR BUILDING—NIGHT,
NEW YORK. 1927.
Oil on canvas. 48×30.
Fisk University, The Alfred
Stieglitz Collection, Nashville.

55. THE RED HILLS WITH SUN.
1927. Oil on canvas. 27×32.
The Phillips Collection,
Washington, D.C.

56. RED POPPY. 1927.
Oil on canvas. 7⅛×9.
Daniel Catton Rich.

*57. SEAWEED. 1927.
Oil on canvas. 9×7.

*58. BROWN AND TAN LEAVES. 1928.
Oil on canvas. 40×30.
Private Collection.

59. EAST RIVER FROM THE
THIRTIETH STORY OF THE
SHELTON HOTEL. 1928.
Oil on canvas. 30×48.
New Britain Museum of American
Art, New Britain, Connecticut.

*60. RIVER, NEW YORK. 1928.
Oil on canvas. 12×32.
Sidney and George Perutz.

*61. THE LAWRENCE TREE. 1929.
Oil on canvas. 30×40.

*62. LAKE GEORGE WINDOW. 1929.
Oil on canvas. 40×30.
The Museum of Modern Art,
New York, acquired through the
Richard D. Brixey Bequest.

*63. BLACK CROSS, NEW MEXICO.
1929. Oil on canvas. 39×30.
The Art Institute of Chicago.

64. CLAM SHELL. 1930.
Oil on canvas. 24×36.
The Metropolitan Museum of Art,
The Alfred Stieglitz Collection.

*65. BLACK AND WHITE. 1930.
Oil on canvas. 36×24.

*66. JACK-IN-THE-PULPIT, NO. 2.
1930. Oil on canvas. 40×30.

*67. JACK-IN-THE-PULPIT, NO. 3.
1930. Oil on canvas. 40×30.

*68. JACK-IN-THE-PULPIT, NO. 4.
1930. Oil on canvas. 40×30.
Dr. Helen W. Boigon.

*69. JACK-IN-THE-PULPIT, NO. 5.
1930. Oil on canvas. 48×30.

*70. JACK-IN-THE-PULPIT, NO. 6.
1930. Oil on canvas. 36×18.

71. DARK MESA AND PINK SKY.
1930. Oil on canvas. 16×29⅞.
Amon Carter Museum of
Western Art, Fort Worth, Texas.

72. RANCHOS CHURCH. 1930.
Oil on canvas. 24×36.
The Metropolitan Museum of Art,
The Alfred Stieglitz Collection.

*73. COW'S SKULL—RED WHITE
AND BLUE. 1931.
Oil on canvas. 40×36.
The Metropolitan Museum of Art,
The Alfred Stieglitz Collection.

74. COW'S SKULL WITH RED.
1931–36. Oil on canvas. 36×40⅛.
National Gallery of Art, The
Alfred Stieglitz Collection, on
loan from Georgia O'Keeffe.

*75. CROSS BY THE SEA, CANADA.
1932. Oil on canvas. 36×24.
The Currier Gallery of Art,
Manchester, New Hampshire.

*76. JIMSON WEED. 1932.
Oil on canvas. 48×40.
Private Collection.

*77. NATURE FORMS, GASPÉ. 1932.
Oil on canvas. 10×24.

*78. WHITE BARN, NO. 1. 1932.
Oil on canvas. 16×30.
Wright Ludington.

*79. THE WHITE TRUMPET FLOWER.
1932. Oil on canvas. 30×40.

*80. BANANA FLOWER. 1933.
Charcoal. 21¾×14¾. The
Museum of Modern Art, New
York, given anonymously 1936.

81. BARN WITH SNOW. 1934.
Oil on canvas. 16×28.
Sidney and George Perutz.

82. DRAWING NO. 40. 1934.
Pencil. 16⅛×11.

*83. PURPLE HILLS NEAR ABIQUIU.
1935. Oil on canvas. 16×30.

84. DEER'S SKULL WITH
PEDERNAL. 1936.
Oil on canvas. 40×30.
William H. Lane Foundation.

*85. SUMMER DAYS. 1936.
Oil on canvas. 36×30.

*86. FROM THE FARAWAY NEARBY.
1937. Oil on canvas. 36×40⅛.
The Metropolitan Museum of Art,
The Alfred Stieglitz Collection.

87. BEAUFORD DELANEY. early
1940's? Charcoal. 24¾×18⅝.

*88. AN ORCHID. 1941.
Pastel. 27×21½ (sight).

89. THE WHITE PLACE IN SHADOW.
1942. Oil on canvas. 30×24.
The Phillips Collection,
Washington, D.C.

*90. THE BLACK PLACE. 1943.
Oil on canvas. 20×36.
The Art Institute of Chicago,
The Alfred Stieglitz Collection.

*91. PELVIS WITH SHADOWS AND
THE MOON. 1943.
Oil on canvas. 40×48¾.
Mrs. Frank Lloyd Wright.

*92. CLIFFS BEYOND ABIQUIU,
DRY WATERFALL. 1943.
Oil on canvas. 30×16.

93. DEAD COTTONWOOD TREE.
1943. Oil on canvas. 36×30.
Santa Barbara Museum of Art,
gift of Mrs. Gary Cooper.

*94. UNTITLED 3. 1944.
Pastel. 27½×21½ (sight).
Mrs. Helen DeVitt Jones.

*95. BLACK PLACE III. 1944.
Oil on canvas. 36×40.

96. PELVIS SERIES, RED WITH
YELLOW. 1945.
Oil on canvas. 36×48.
Mrs. Charles David Tandy.

97. RED HILLS AND SKY. 1945.
Oil on canvas. 30×40.
Private Collection.

*98. SPRING TREE NO. II. 1945.
Oil on canvas. 30×36.
Private Collection.

*99. A BLACK BIRD WITH SNOW-
COVERED RED HILLS. 1946.
Oil on canvas. 36×48.
Susan and David Workman.

*100. IN THE PATIO I. 1946.
Oil on paper. 30×24.
Mr. and Mrs. Norton S.
Walbridge.

101. SPRING. 1948.
Oil on canvas. 48×84.
Mr. and Mrs. J. Carrington
Woolley.

*102. BLACK PLACE GREEN. 1949.
Oil on canvas. 38×48.

*103. RED TREE, YELLOW SKY. 1952.
Oil on canvas. 30×48.
William H. Lane Foundation.

*104. ANTELOPE. 1954.
Oil on canvas. 14×32.
Mr. and Mrs. Stanley Marcus.

105. ANTELOPE HORNS. 1954.
Pencil. 19×24.
Mrs. Frank Sebring.

*106. WINTER COTTONWOODS
EAST, V. 1954.
Oil on canvas. 40×36.
Private Collection.

*107. FROM THE PLAINS, II. 1954.
Oil on canvas. 48×72.
Susan and David Workman.

108. GREEN PATIO DOOR. 1955.
Oil on canvas. 30×20.
Albright-Knox Art Gallery,
Buffalo, New York, gift of
Seymour H. Knox.

109. BLACK PATIO DOOR. 1955.
Oil on canvas. 40⅛×30.
Amon Carter Museum of
Western Art, Fort Worth, Texas.

*110. LADDER TO THE MOON. 1958.
Oil on canvas. 40×30.

111. DRAWING NO. III. 1959.
Charcoal. 18⅝×24⅝.

*112. DRAWING NO. X. 1959.
Charcoal. 24⅝×18⅝.

*113. WHITE PATIO WITH RED
DOOR. 1960.
Oil on canvas. 48×84.

114. IT WAS RED AND PINK. 1959.
Oil on canvas. 30×40.
Bradley Family Foundation Inc.,
gift of Mrs. Harry Lynde Bradley.

*115. IT WAS BLUE AND GREEN.
1960. Oil on canvas. 30×40.
Lawrence H. Bloedel.

116. SKY ABOVE WHITE CLOUDS I.
1962. Oil on canvas. 60×80.

*117. SKY ABOVE CLOUDS III. 1963.
Oil on canvas. 48×84.
Private Collection.

*118. THE WINTER ROAD. 1963.
Oil on canvas. 22×18.

*119. ROAD PAST THE VIEW. 1964.
Oil on canvas. 24¼×30⅛.

*120. SKY ABOVE CLOUDS IV. 1965.
Oil on canvas. 96×288.
(See cover.)

*121. BLACK ROCK WITH BLUE, III.
1970. Oil on canvas. 20×17.

# Illustrations

1. BLUE LINES. 1916. Watercolor. 25×19.
   The Metropolitan Museum of Art, The Alfred Stieglitz Collection.

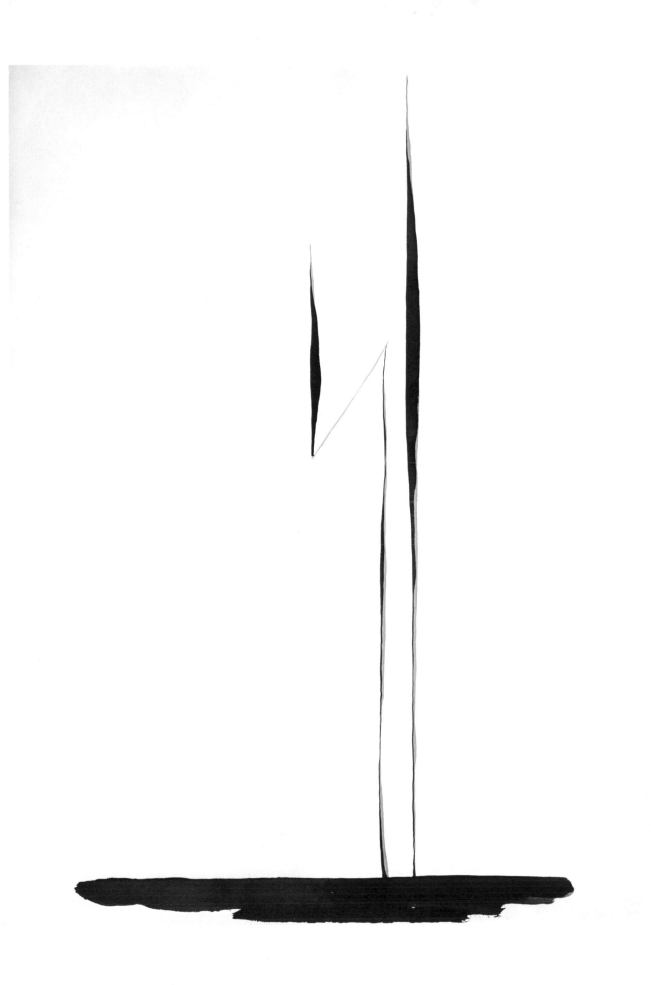

3. DRAWING NO. 13. 1915. Charcoal. 24¾ × 18⅞.
The Metropolitan Museum of Art, The Alfred Stieglitz Collection.

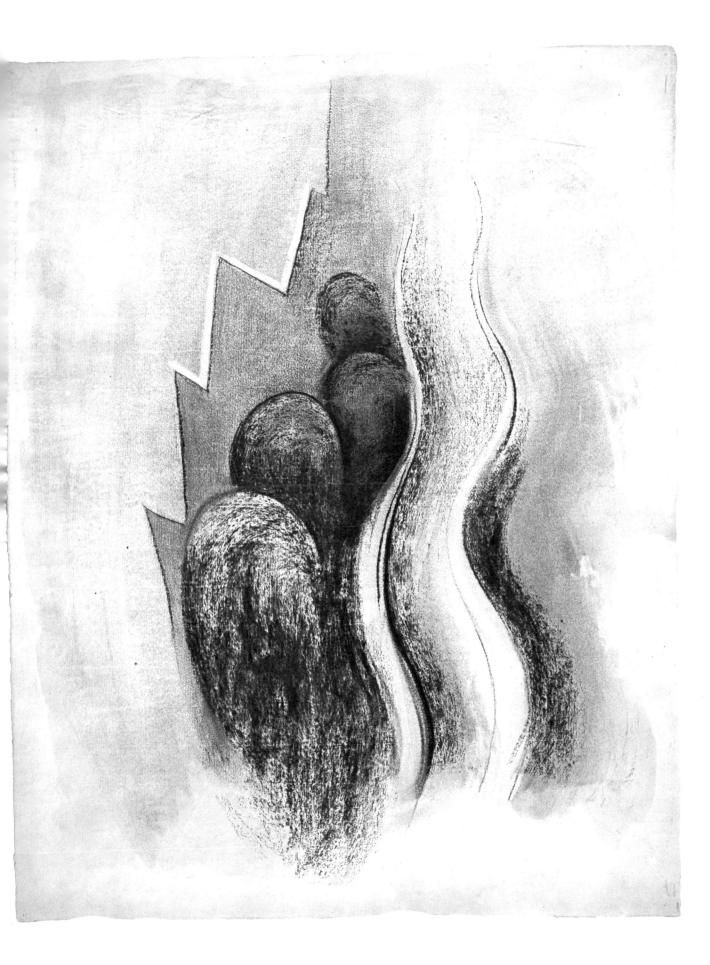

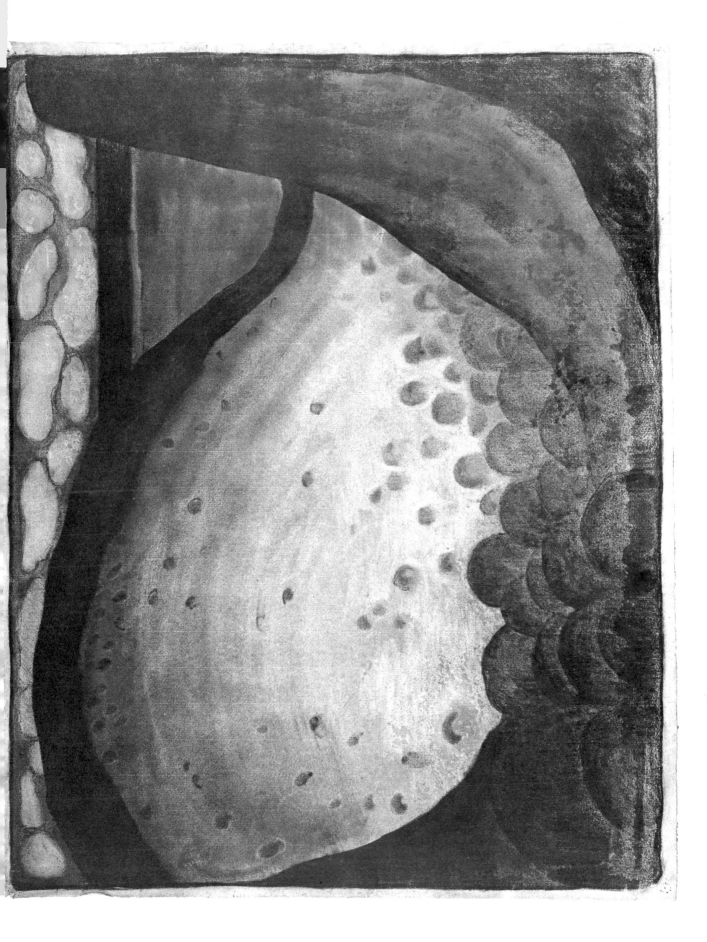

7. BLUE NO. II. 1916. Watercolor. 15 7/8 × 11. The Brooklyn Museum.

12. PAINTING NO. 22. 1916. Oil on board. 12 7/8 × 17 1/4.

15. EVENING STAR NO. IV . 1917. Watercolor. 9 × 12.

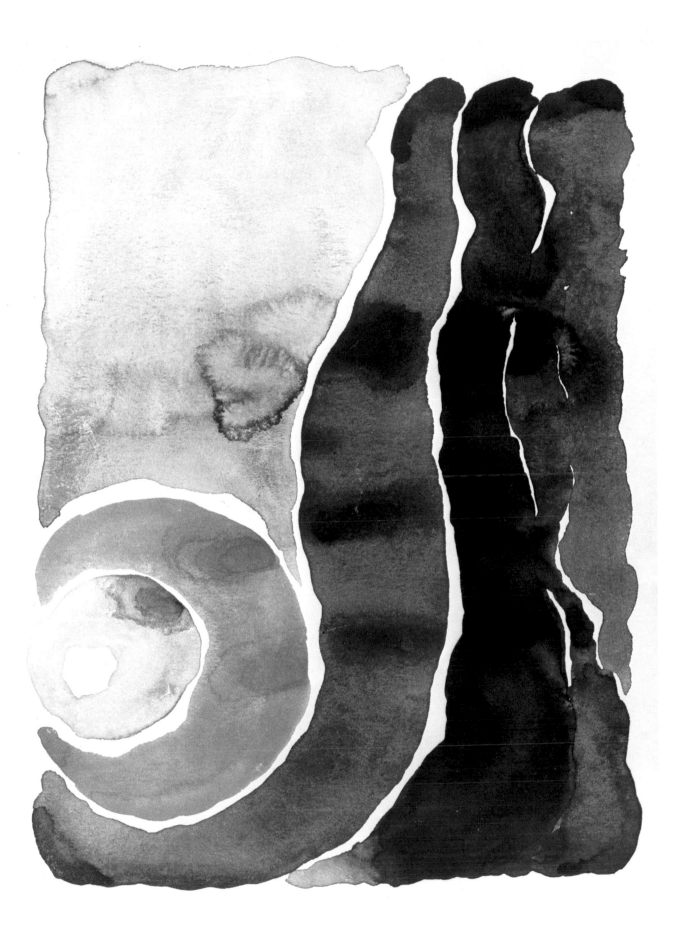

18. LIGHT COMING ON THE PLAINS NO. II. 1917. Watercolor. 12×9.
Amon Carter Museum of Western Art, Fort Worth, Texas.

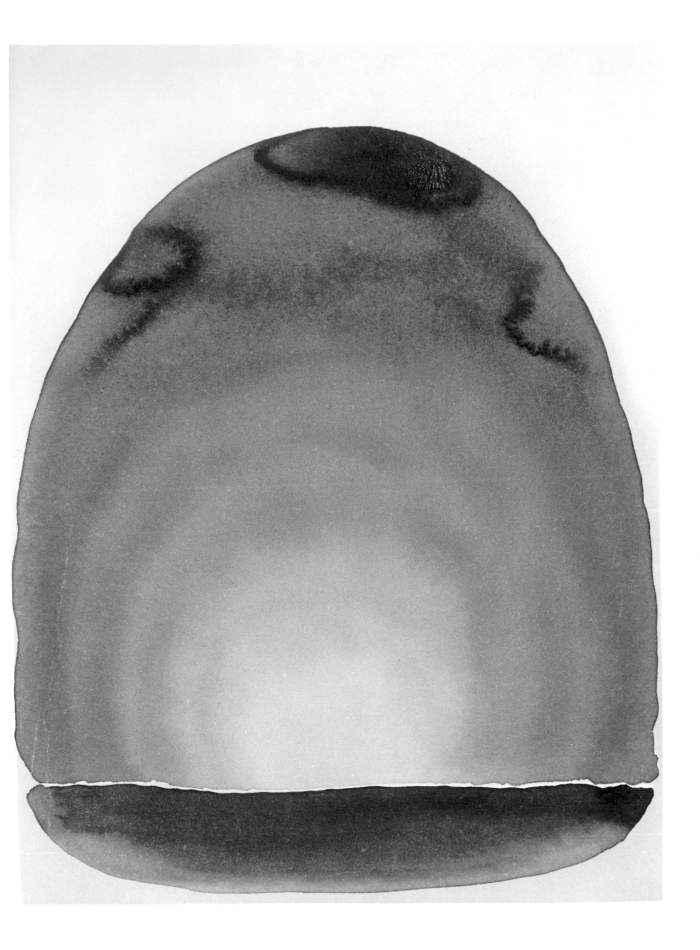

21. ORANGE AND RED STREAK. 1919. Oil on canvas. 27×25.

22. BLACK SPOT NO. 3. 1919. Oil on canvas. 24×16.

23. BLUE AND GREEN MUSIC. 1919. Oil on canvas. 23 × 19.
The Art Institute of Chicago, The Alfred Stieglitz Collection.

24. MUSIC—PINK AND BLUE NO. 1. 1919. Oil on canvas. 35×29.

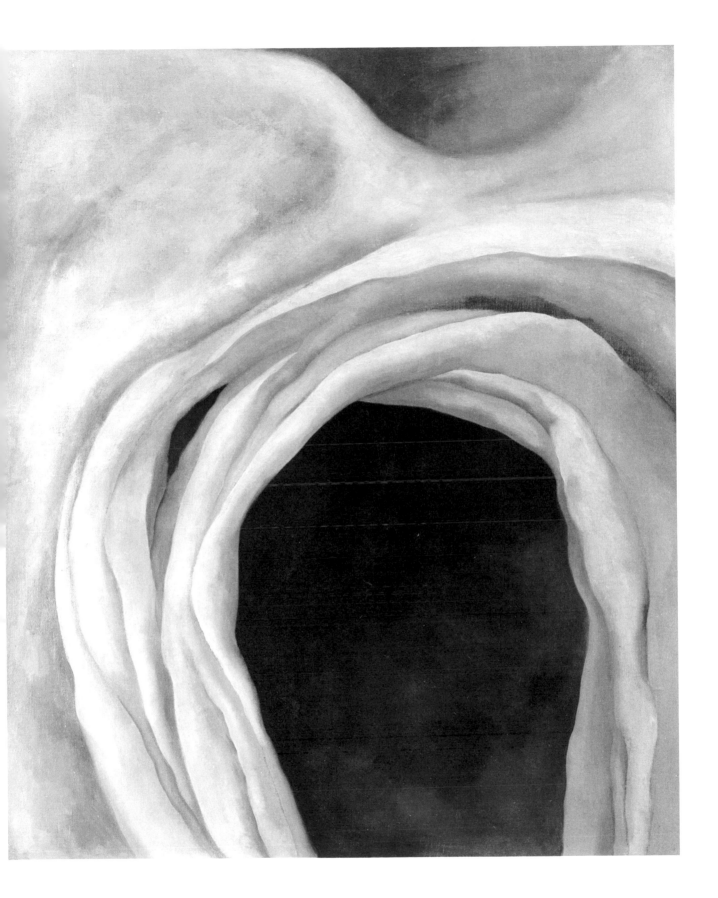

25. 59TH STREET STUDIO. 1919. Oil on canvas. 35×29.

26. SERIES I, NO. 12. 1920. Oil on canvas. 20×17.

27. LAKE GEORGE WITH CROWS. C. 1921. Oil on canvas. 28 1/2 × 25.

31. GREY LINE WITH BLACK, BLUE AND YELLOW. c. 1923. Oil on canvas. 48×30.

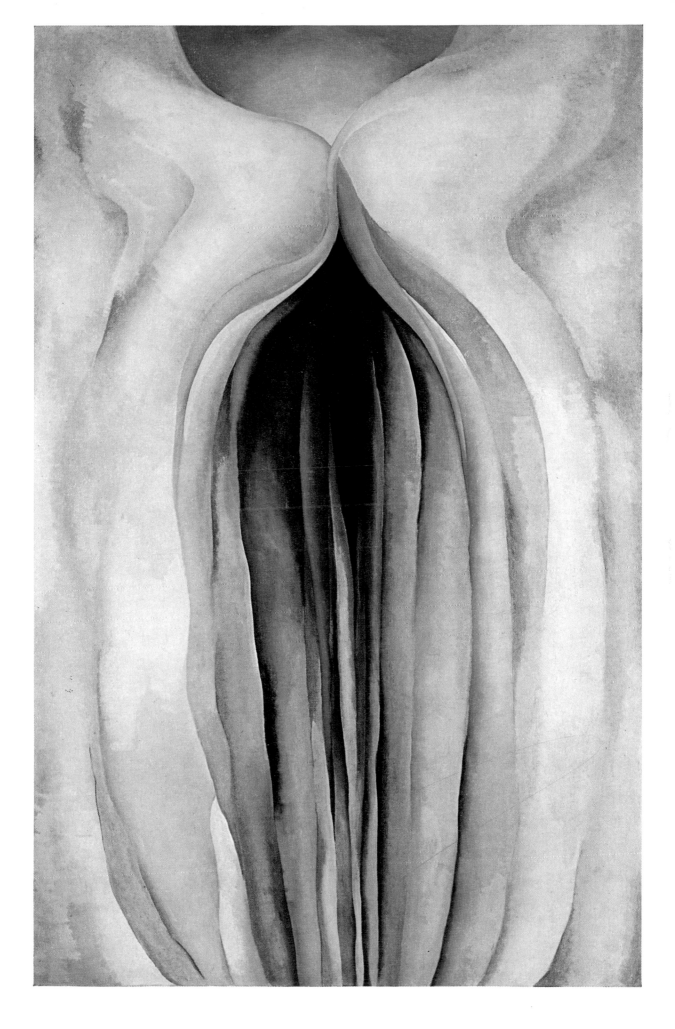

32. DARK ABSTRACTION. 1924. Oil on canvas. 24 7/8 × 20 7/8.
City Art Museum of St. Louis.

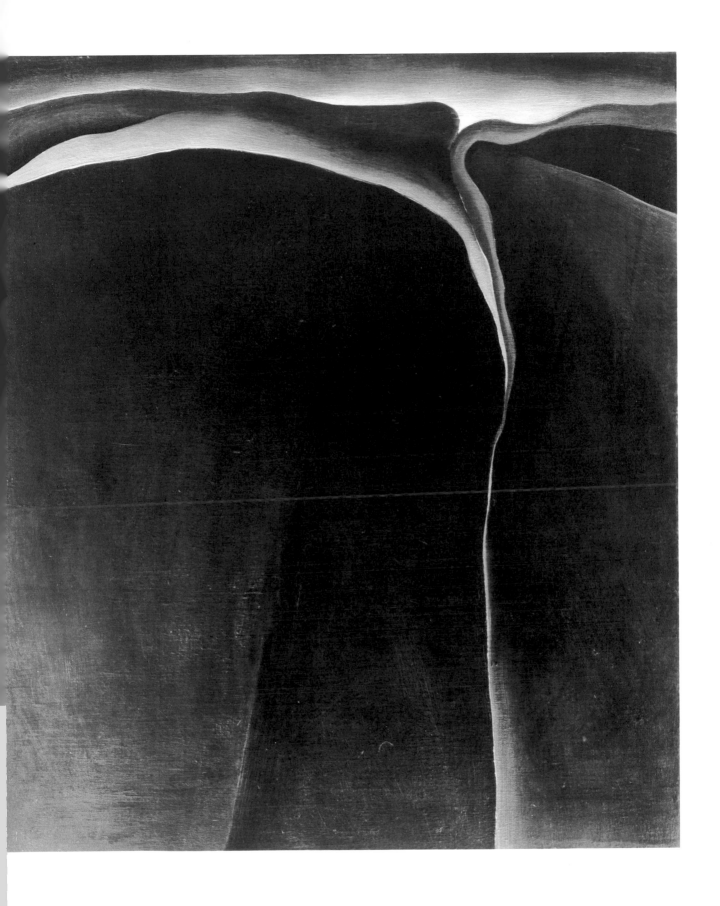

33. FLOWER ABSTRACTION. 1924. Oil on canvas. 48×30.

34. FROM THE LAKE NO. 3. 1924. Oil on canvas. 36×30.

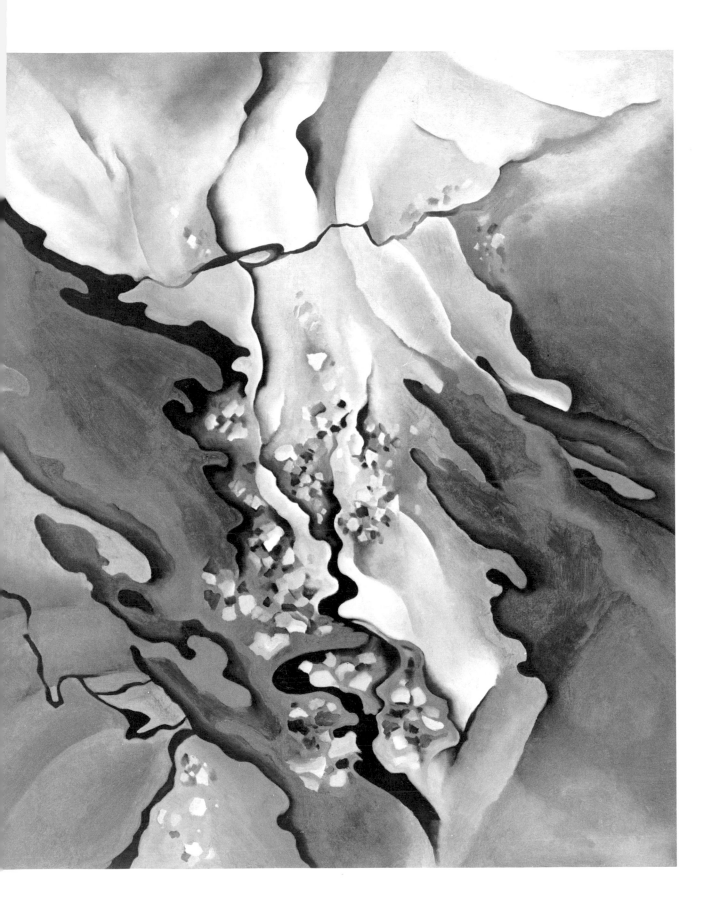

36. RED YELLOW AND BLACK STREAK. 1924. Oil on canvas. 39½×32.

38. GREY TREE, LAKE GEORGE. 1925. Oil on canvas. 36×30.

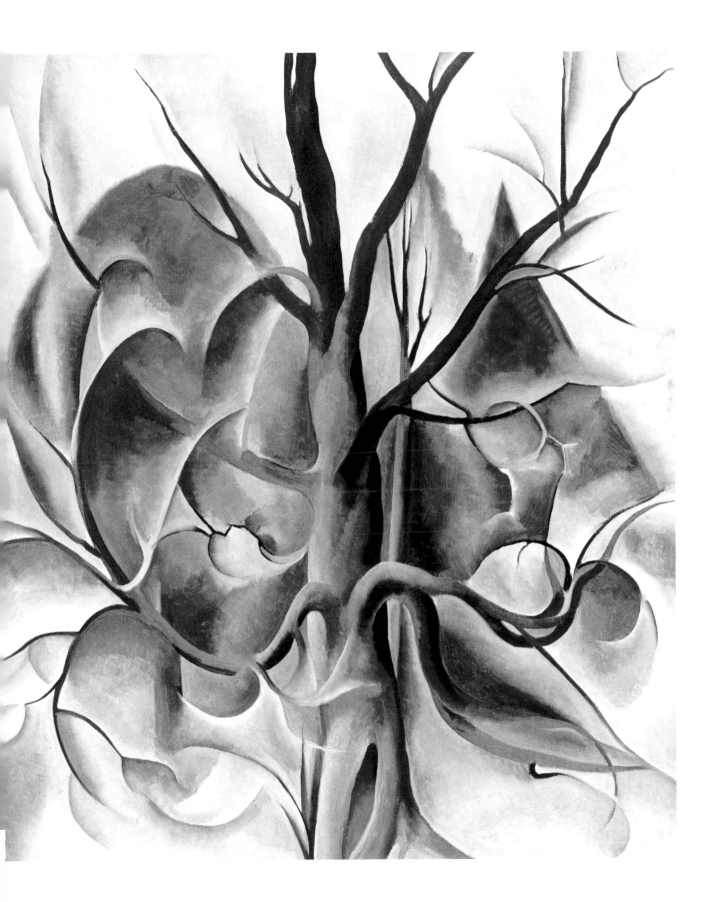

39. ABSTRACTION. 1926. Oil on canvas. 30×18.
Whitney Museum of American Art.

40. BLACK IRIS. 1926. Oil on canvas. 36×30.
   The Metropolitan Museum of Art, The Alfred Stieglitz Collection.

41. CLOSED CLAM SHELL. 1926. Oil on canvas. 20×9.
    Private Collection.

42. OPEN CLAM SHELL. 1926. Oil on canvas. 20×9.
    Private Collection.

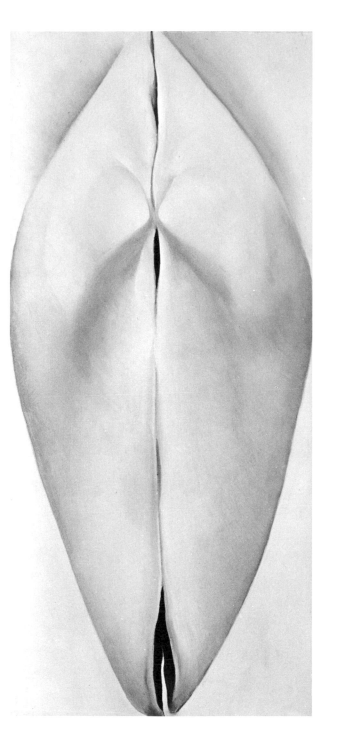
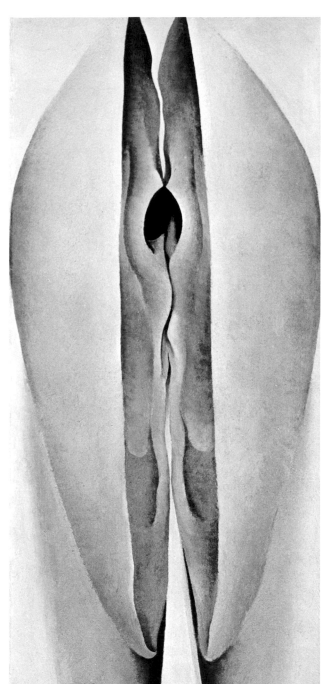

44. SHELL AND OLD SHINGLE II. 1926. Oil on canvas. 30✕18.

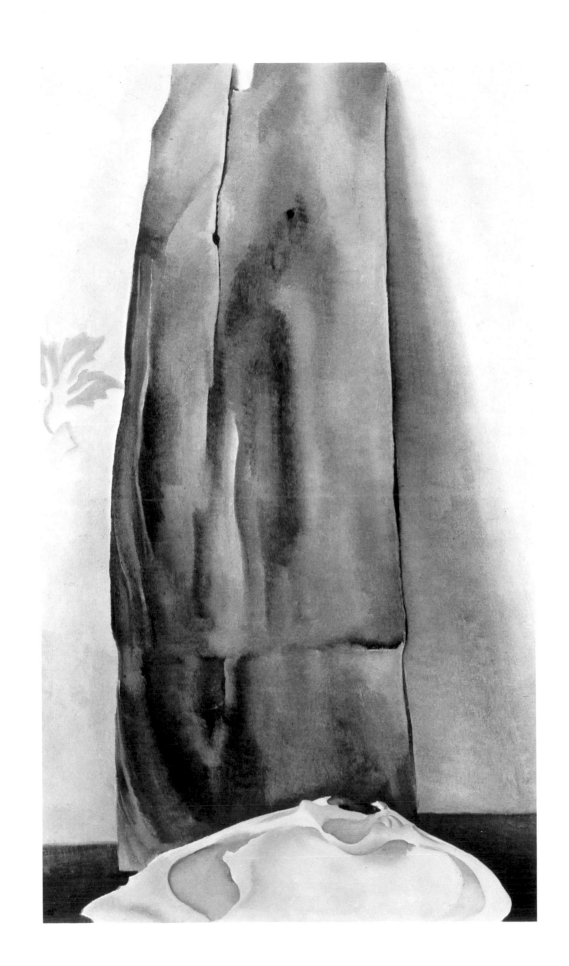

47. SHELL AND OLD SHINGLE VI. 1926. Oil on canvas. 30× 18.
Mr. and Mrs. Charles E. Claggett.

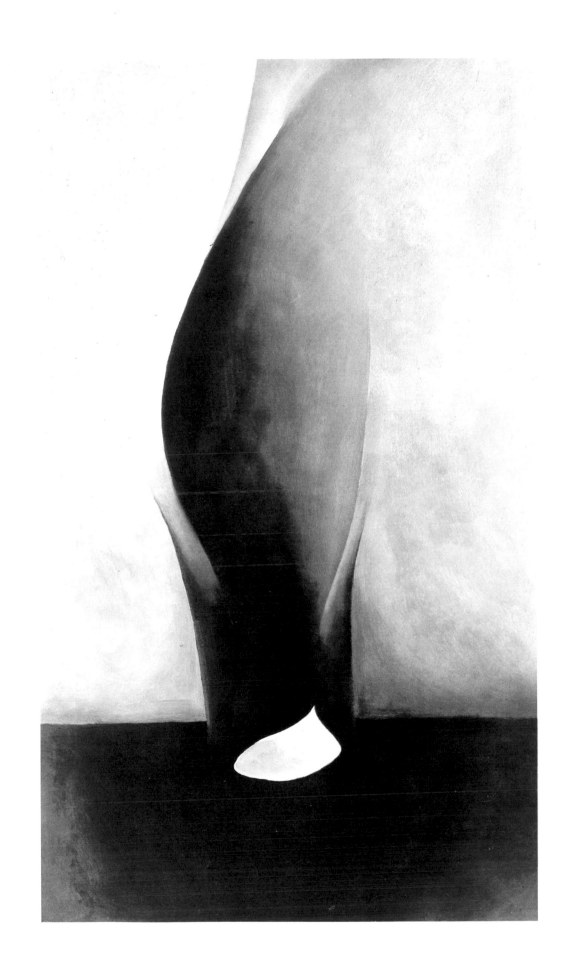

49. THE SHELTON WITH SUNSPOTS. 1926. Oil on canvas. 48 5/8 × 30 5/8. Inland Steel Company.

50. ABSTRACTION—WHITE ROSE II. 1927. Oil on canvas. 36×30. Private Collection.

52. BLACK ABSTRACTION. 1927. Oil on canvas. 30 × 40¼.
The Metropolitan Museum of Art, The Alfred Stieglitz Collection.

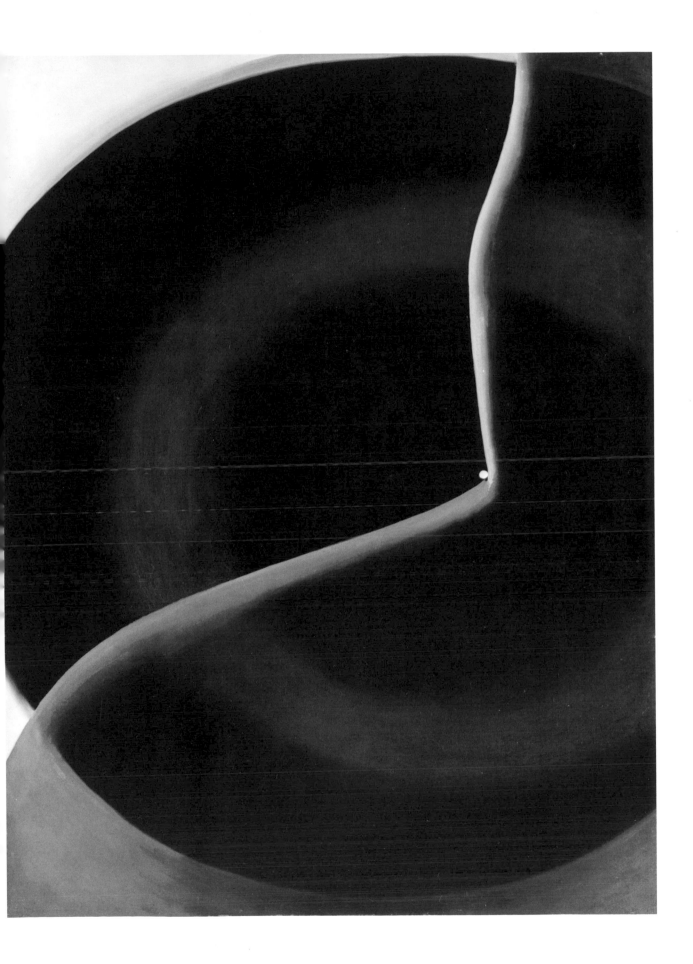

54. RADIATOR BUILDING—NIGHT, NEW YORK. 1927. Oil on canvas. 48×30.
Fisk University, The Alfred Stieglitz Collection, Nashville.

57. SEAWEED. 1927. Oil on canvas. 9×7.

58. BROWN AND TAN LEAVES. 1928. Oil on canvas. 40×30.
Private Collection.

60. RIVER, NEW YORK. 1928. Oil on canvas. 12×32. Sidney and George Perutz.

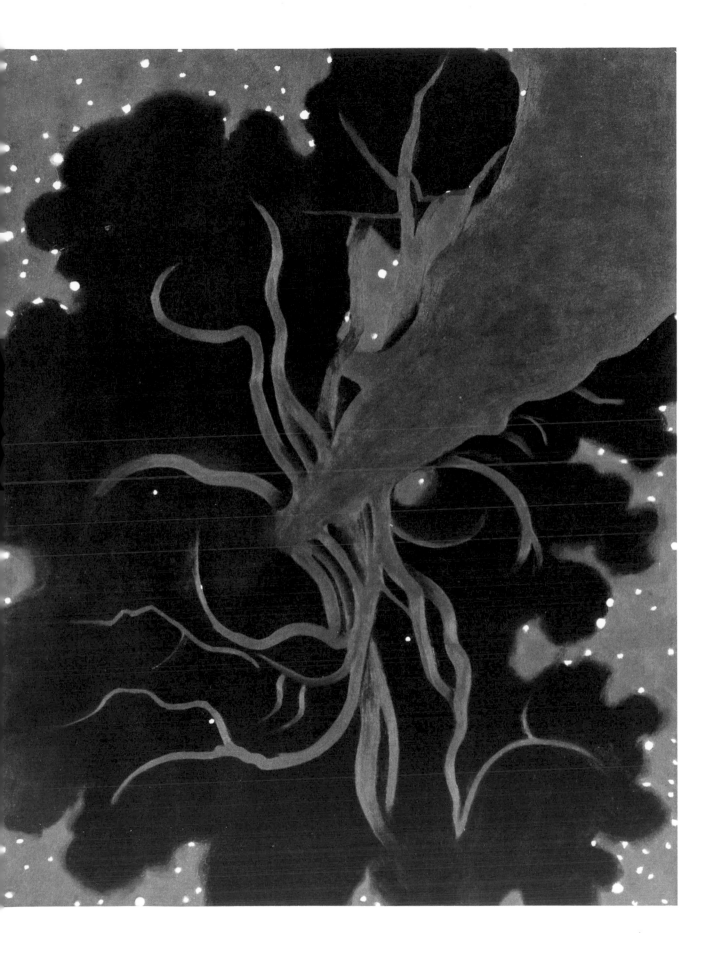

62. LAKE GEORGE WINDOW. 1929. Oil on canvas. 40× 30.
The Museum of Modern Art, New York.

63. BLACK CROSS, NEW MEXICO. Oil on canvas. 1929. 39×30.
   The Art Institute of Chicago.

65. BLACK AND WHITE. 1930. Oil on canvas. 36×24.

66. JACK-IN-THE-PULPIT, NO. 2. 1930. Oil on canvas. 40 × 30.

67. JACK-IN-THE-PULPIT, NO. 3. 1930. Oil on canvas. 40×30.

68. JACK-IN-THE-PULPIT, NO. 4. 1930. Oil on canvas. 40×30.
Dr. Helen W. Boigon.

69. JACK-IN-THE-PULPIT, NO. 5. 1930. Oil on canvas. 48×30.

70. JACK-IN-THE-PULPIT, NO. 6. 1930. Oil on canvas. 36×18.

73. COW'S SKULL—RED WHITE AND BLUE. 1931. Oil on canvas. 40×36. The Metropolitan Museum of Art, The Alfred Stieglitz Collection.

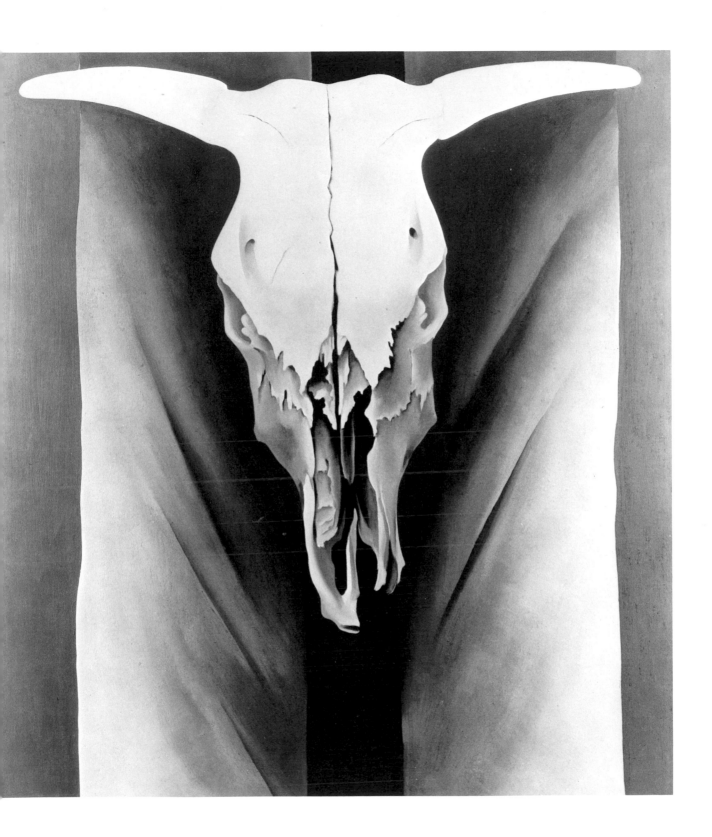

75. CROSS BY THE SEA, CANADA. 1932. Oil on canvas. 36×24.
The Currier Gallery of Art, Manchester, New Hampshire.

76. JIMSON WEED. 1932. Oil on canvas. 48×40.
    Private Collection.

77. NATURE FORMS, GASPÉ. 1932. Oil on canvas. 10×24.

78. WHITE BARN, NO. 1. 1932. Oil on canvas. 16×30.
Wright Ludington.

79. THE WHITE TRUMPET FLOWER. 1932. Oil on canvas. 30×40.

80. BANANA FLOWER. 1933. Charcoal. 21 ¾ × 14 ¾.
The Museum of Modern Art, New York.

83. PURPLE HILLS NEAR ABIQUIU. 1935. Oil on canvas. 16×30.

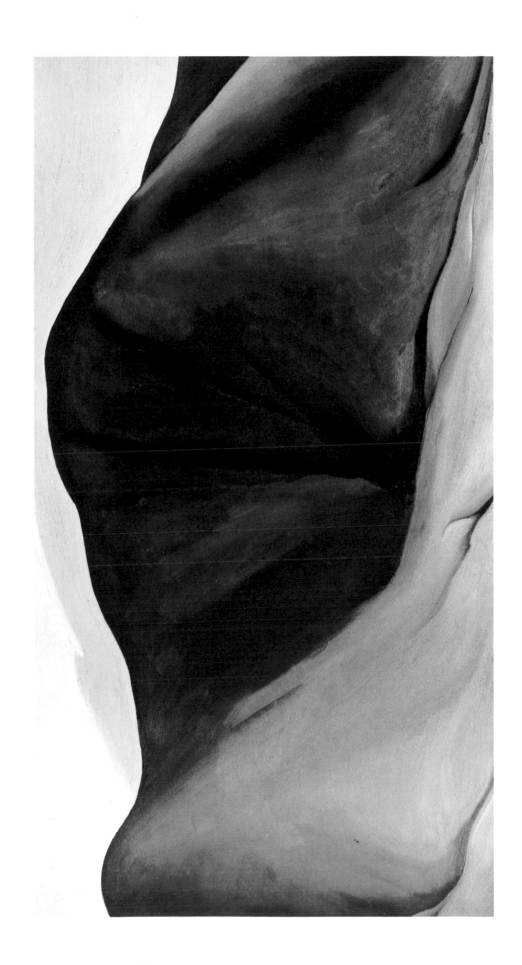

85. SUMMER DAYS. 1936. Oil on canvas. 36×30.

86. FROM THE FARAWAY NEARBY. 1937. Oil on canvas. 36 × 40⅛.
   The Metropolitan Museum of Art, The Alfred Stieglitz Collection.

88. AN ORCHID. 1941. Pastel. 27×21 ½ (sight).

90. THE BLACK PLACE. 1943. Oil on canvas. 20×36.
The Art Institute of Chicago, The Alfred Stieglitz Collection.

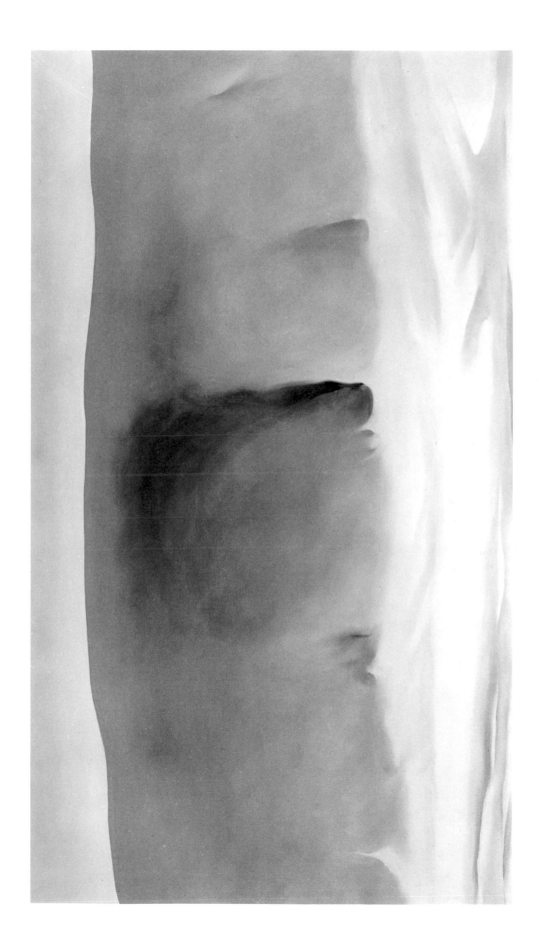

91. PELVIS WITH SHADOWS AND THE MOON. 1943. Oil on canvas. 40×48 ¾. Mrs. Frank Lloyd Wright.

92. CLIFFS BEYOND ABIQUIU, DRY WATERFALL. 1943. Oil on canvas. 30×16.

94. UNTITLED 3. 1944. Pastel. 27½×21½ (sight).
Mrs. Helen DeVitt Jones.

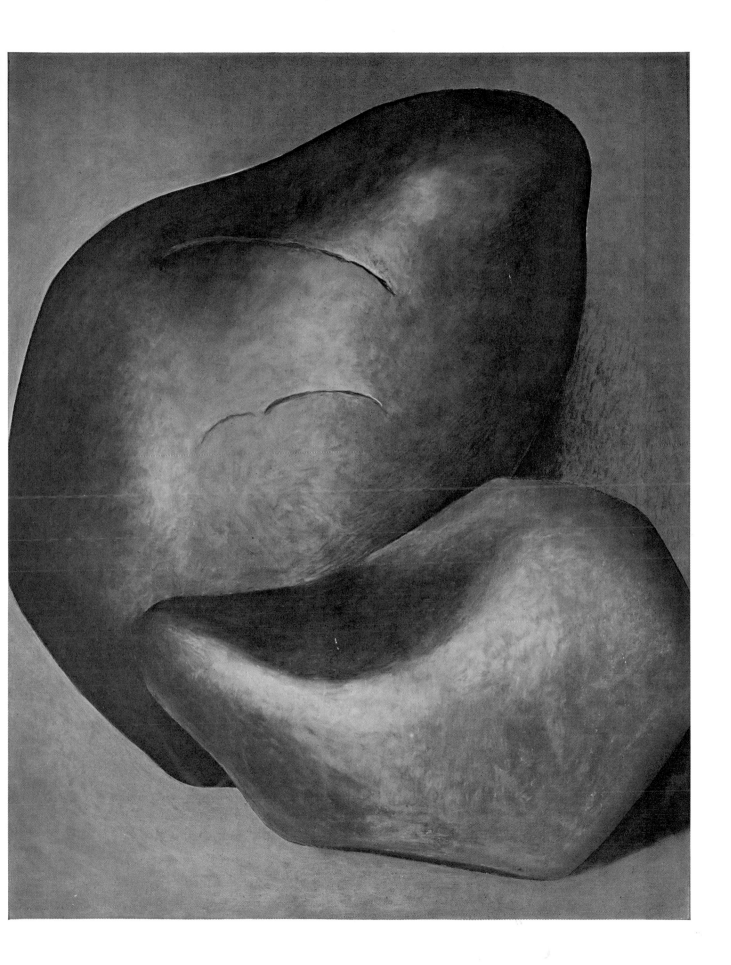

95. BLACK PLACE III. 1944. Oil on canvas. 36×40.

98. SPRING TREE NO. II. 1945. Oil on canvas. 30×36.
Private Collection.

99. A BLACK BIRD WITH SNOW-COVERED RED HILLS. 1946. Oil on canvas. 36×48.
Susan and David Workman.

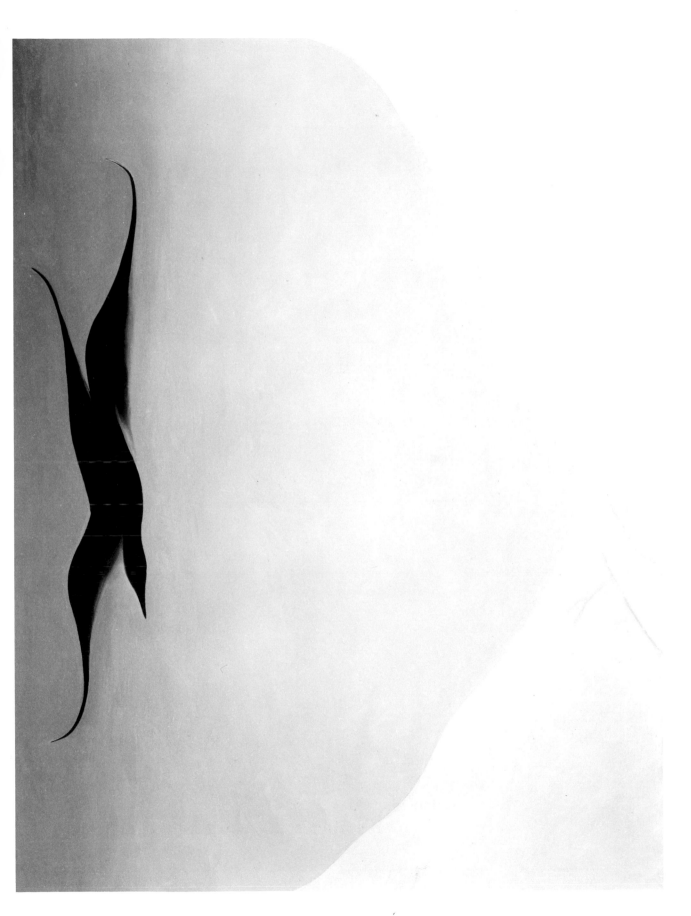

100. IN THE PATIO I. 1946. Oil on paper. 30×24.
Mr. and Mrs. Norton S. Walbridge.

102. BLACK PLACE GREEN. 1949. Oil on canvas. 38×48.

103. RED TREE, YELLOW SKY. 1952. Oil on canvas. 30×48. William H. Lane Foundation.

104. ANTELOPE. 1954. Oil on canvas. 14 × 32.
Mr. and Mrs. Stanley Marcus.

106. WINTER COTTONWOODS EAST, V. 1954. Oil on canvas. 40 × 36. Private Collection.

107. FROM THE PLAINS II. 1954. Oil on canvas. 48×72. Susan and David Workman.

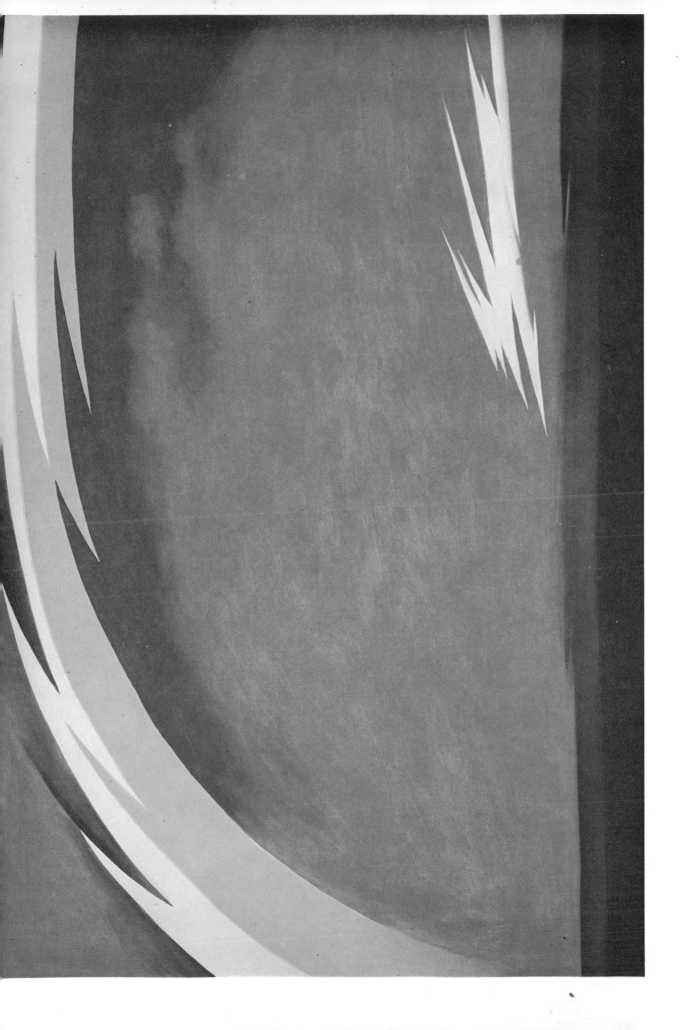

110. LADDER TO THE MOON. 1958. Oil on canvas. 40×30.

112. DRAWING NO. X. 1959. Charcoal. 24 5/8 × 18 5/8.

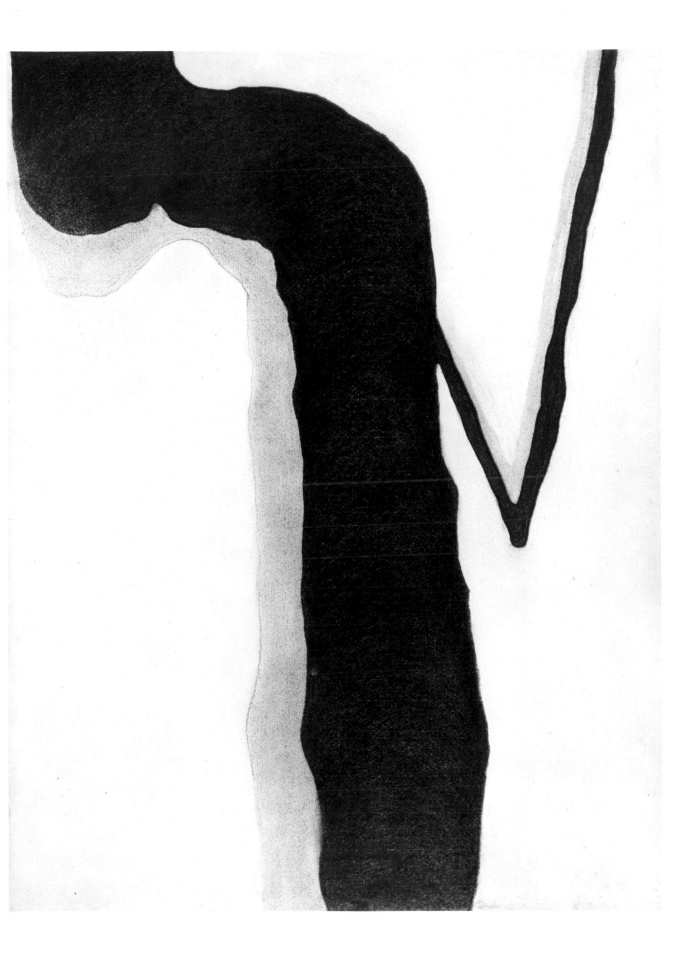

113. WHITE PATIO WITH RED DOOR. 1960. Oil on canvas. 48×84.

115. IT WAS BLUE AND GREEN. 1960. Oil on canvas. 30 × 40.
Lawrence H. Bloedel.

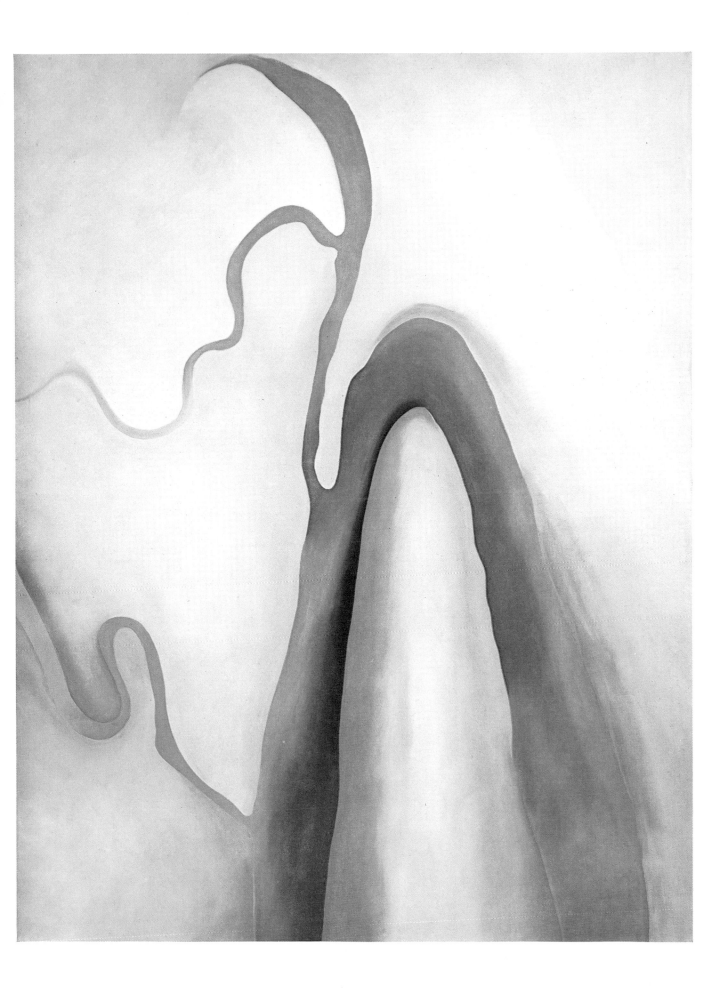

117. SKY ABOVE CLOUDS III. 1963. Oil on canvas. 48×84. Private Collection.

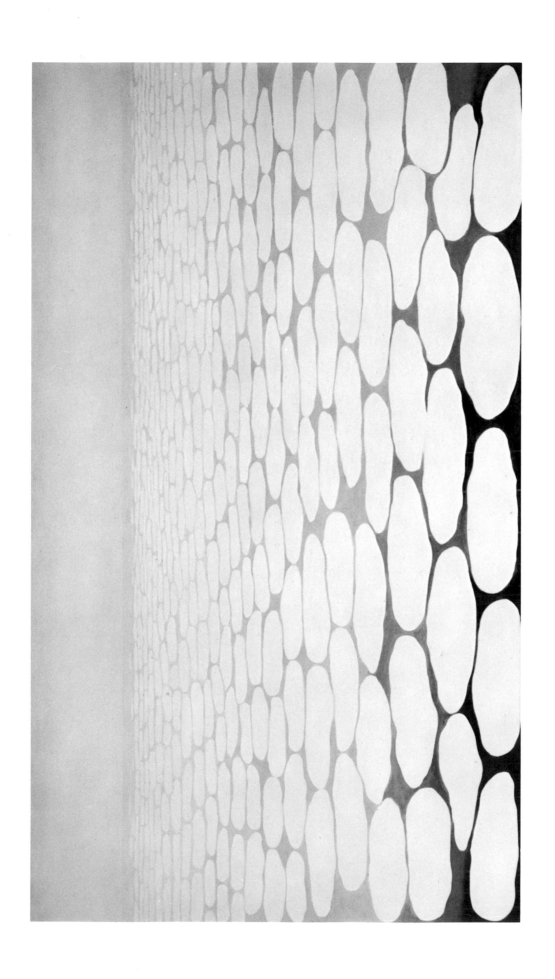

118. THE WINTER ROAD. 1963. Oil on canvas. 22×18.

119. ROAD PAST THE VIEW. 1964. Oil on canvas. 24 1/4 × 30 1/8.

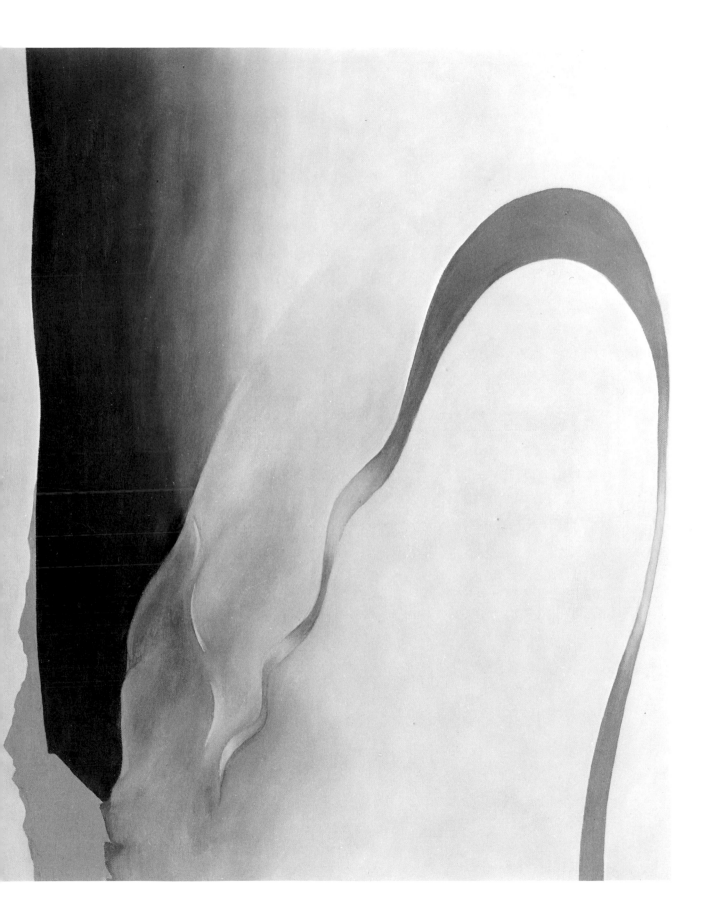

121. BLACK ROCK WITH BLUE, III. 1970. Oil on canvas. 20×17.

# Chronology

**1887–1905**   Georgia O'Keeffe was born near Sun Prairie, Wisconsin, November 15, 1887, the daughter of Francis and Ida (Totto) O'Keeffe, the second child of seven brothers and sisters. Her childhood was spent on the family's 600-acre farm. Early schooling was in a nearby country school, then in Madison, Wisconsin, with her last two years of high school spent at Chatham Episcopal Institute, Chatham, Virginia.

Decision to become an artist was made at the age of ten. Along with two younger sisters, had weekly private drawing lessons at the ages of eleven and twelve, until regular instruction at the convent in Madison and in high school.

Family moved to Williamsburg, Virginia, in 1902.

**1905–06**   Attended Art Institute of Chicago, where she studied with John Vanderpoel, whom she remembers as the teacher there who was most important to her.

Long illness, typhoid fever, and recuperation in Williamsburg.

**1907–08**   Attended Art Students League, New York, where she studied with William M. Chase, F. Luis Mora, and Kenyon Cox.

Visit to the Rodin exhibition at Alfred Stieglitz's gallery, *291*, along with other students. Was awarded Chase Still Life Scholarship – result of which was part of summer at the League Outdoor School at Lake George, New York.

**1908–12**   Decided to give up painting.

Went to Chicago, where she held two jobs in commercial art, drawing lace and embroidery for advertisements. A case of measles, and its effect on her eyes, caused her to give up this work. Meanwhile, mother's illness had caused the family to move to Charlottesville, Virginia.

Summer, 1912. Visited art class at University of Virginia given by Alon Bement, a teacher under Arthur Dow. This led to a renewed interest in painting.

Autumn, 1912. Started teaching in Amarillo, Texas, as supervisor of art in the public schools. Kept this job for two years.

**1913**   Summer (also the summers of 1914–1916), taught at the University of Virginia Art Department.

1914–15 Autumn, 1914. Went to New York to study with Arthur Dow at Teachers College, Columbia University, at Alon Bement's suggestion.

Autumn, 1915, took a new teaching position at Columbia College, Columbia, South Carolina, in order to have more time for her own work. Held an exhibition for herself of her work in her room, and saw that every painting was affected by one or another of her teachers. Decided to start over, working on ideas only her own, to please only herself, and began in black and white, charcoal on paper. These drawings she sent to a friend in New York, Anita Pollitzer, with instructions to show them to no one. Her friend, much excited, took them to Alfred Stieglitz, who was so interested that he kept them and, after several months, decided to exhibit them.

1916 February, 1916, returned to Teachers College for spring semester.

May, 1916. Exhibition of early drawings and watercolors at *291* (along with paintings by Charles Duncan and René Lafferty), without O'Keeffe's knowledge, and before she and Stieglitz knew one another. Stieglitz and O'Keeffe first met when she heard that her drawings were on view and went to *291* to make him take them down. The drawings stayed up for May, June and July.

Summer, 1916. Taught once more at the University of Virginia. Correspondence with Stieglitz, who photographed the drawings and sent her the prints.

Autumn, 1916. Position as head of art department at West Texas State Normal School, Canyon, Texas, where she taught for most of the next two years. Continued to paint for herself—mostly drawings and watercolors.

1917 Stieglitz entered two drawings in Society of Independent Artists exhibition.

May, 1917. Stieglitz held the first show of O'Keeffe work alone at *291*, as the gallery's final exhibition. Hearing from Stieglitz that he was ending *291*, O'Keeffe went to New York during her June vacation for a week to see the place for the last time. Found it closed, but Stieglitz re-hung her show for her. First photographs of O'Keeffe by Stieglitz made at this time.

Returned to Texas for summer teaching. That fall, went on vacation trip she had promised to a younger sister, Claudia, who chose to go to Colorado. A detour caused by the washout of bridges took them through New Mexico – O'Keeffe's first glimpse of the area.

1918 Became ill and took leave of absence from teaching. Spent spring in San Antonio, Texas. To New York in early summer at Stieglitz's suggestion, who then offered her a year there in which to paint for herself. At end of summer she resigned the position with West Texas, in order to stay East and paint.

| 1918–28 | Life as a painter, in New York (city) and at Lake George. Visits to Maine during several of these summers. |
|---|---|
| 1923 | Exhibition presented by Stieglitz at the Anderson Galleries of one hundred pictures by Georgia O'Keeffe. |
| 1924 | First big flower paintings. |
| | Exhibition presented by Stieglitz at the Anderson Galleries of fifty-one recent pictures, was held simultaneously with that of his own photographs. |
| | Married Stieglitz. |
| 1925 | "Seven Americans" exhibition, held by Stieglitz at the Anderson Galleries. First exhibition as a group of the American painters he remained closest to over succeeding years (Charles Demuth, Arthur G. Dove, Marsden Hartley, John Marin, and Georgia O'Keeffe), along with the work of two photographers as co-workers in American art--himself and Paul Strand. |
| 1926 | First paintings of the city, New York. |
| 1926–29 | Yearly exhibitions of new work at Stieglitz's Intimate Gallery. |
| 1927 | Retrospective exhibition at The Brooklyn Museum. |
| 1929 | Summer trip to New Mexico with Rebecca Strand. Stayed in Taos with Mabel Dodge Luhan. From this time on, for the most part spent summers in New Mexico, other seasons with Stieglitz in New York and at Lake George. |
| 1930–46 | Yearly exhibitions of new work presented by Stieglitz at his gallery, An American Place. |
| 1931 | First bone paintings. |
| 1932 | Summer trip to Gaspé country. Paintings of Canadian barns and crosses. |
| 1934 | To Bermuda. To New Mexico, first summer at Ghost Ranch, north of Abiquiu. O'Keeffe returned there in 1935 to house which she bought in 1940. |
| 1939 | Travel to Hawaii, for Dole Pineapple Company. |
| | Chosen one of twelve most outstanding women of past fifty years by the New York World's Fair Tomorrow Committee. |
| 1943 | Retrospective exhibition, Art Institute of Chicago, with monograph by Daniel Catton Rich. First full-scale retrospective. |
| 1945 | Bought house in Abiquiu. |

1946    Retrospective exhibition. Museum of Modern Art, New York, presented by James Johnson Sweeney.

Alfred Stieglitz died.

1947–49    Work in New York on the Alfred Stieglitz Estate, and preparing two exhibitions of his Collections. These were held in 1947 at the Museum of Modern Art, New York, and in 1948 at the Art Institute of Chicago.

Summers in New Mexico. Began to live in Abiquiu house in the fall of 1949, shortly before trip to Fisk University (Nashville, Tennessee) for installation of its Alfred Stieglitz Collection.

Elected to the National Institute of Arts and Letters.

1950    Exhibition of new paintings at An American Place. Final exhibition there.

1951    First trip to Mexico.

1952    First one-man exhibition at Downtown Gallery, New York, of work in pastel. Other one-man shows there in 1955 and 1961 of new paintings, and in 1958 of early watercolors. Withdrew paintings from Downtown Gallery in 1963.

1953–1969    *Travel.* First trip to Europe – to France and to Spain, in 1953. Return to Spain for three months in 1954. Travel to Peru in 1956, for three months along coast and then high Andes country. In 1959, trip around the world for three months, including seven weeks in India. (Paintings from above the clouds began after this trip.) 1960, went to Japan, Formosa, the Philippines, Hong Kong, Southeast Asia and some South Pacific islands. 1961, first of numerous trips down the Colorado River. 1963, travel to Greece, Egypt, and the Near East. 1966, travel to England and Austria. 1967, again down the Colorado River. 1969, travel again down the Colorado, and to Vienna to see the Lipizzan horses a second time.

1960    Retrospective exhibition, Worcester Art Museum (Worcester, Massachusetts).

1963    Elected to American Academy of Arts and Letters.

Received Brandeis University Creative Arts Award.

1965    Painted mural, SKY ABOVE CLOUDS IV, eight by twenty-four feet.

1966    Retrospective exhibition, Amon Carter Museum of Western Art (Fort Worth); Museum of Fine Arts (Houston); and University of New Mexico Art Museum (Albuquerque).

Elected to American Academy of Arts and Sciences.

1970    Awarded the National Institute of Arts and Letters' Gold Medal for Painting.

# Principal Exhibitions of Paintings

## AT THE GALLERIES OF ALFRED STIEGLITZ

### Photo-Secession Galleries (291)
1917 April. Oils, watercolors, drawings, sculpture

### Anderson Galleries (arranged by Stieglitz)
1923 January–February. One hundred oils, watercolors, pastels, and drawings

1924 March. Fifty-one recent pictures

### The Intimate Gallery
1926 February–March. Fifty recent paintings

1927 January–February. Forty new paintings

1928 January–February. Forty new paintings

1929 February–March. Forty new paintings

### An American Place
1930 February–March. New Paintings. New Mexico, New York, Lake George

1931 January–February. Recent paintings. New Mexico, New York

1932 December (1931)–February. 33 New Paintings. New Mexico

1933 January–February. Paintings. New and Some Old

1934 January–March. 44 Selected Paintings (1915–1927)

1935 January–March. Paintings (1919–1934)

1936 January–February. Recent paintings. 1935

1937 February–March. New Paintings.

1938 December (1937)–February. Annual exhibition of new paintings

1939 January–March. Annual exhibition of new paintings

1940 February–March. Annual exhibition of new paintings

1941 January–March. New paintings

1942 February–March. Recent paintings

1943 March–May. Annual exhibition of new paintings

1944 January–March. Paintings, 1943

1945 January–March. Paintings, 1944

1946 February–March. Annual exhibition of new paintings

1950 October–November. Paintings, 1946–1950

## AT THE DOWNTOWN GALLERY

1952 February–March. Paintings in pastel, 1914–1945

1955 March–April. New Paintings

1958 February–March. Watercolors, 1916–1917

1961 April–May. Paintings and drawings, 1957–1961

## MAJOR RETROSPECTIVE EXHIBITIONS

1943 January–February. Art Institute of Chicago, Chicago, Illinois

1946 May–August. Museum of Modern Art, New York, New York

1960 October–December. Worcester Art Museum, Worcester, Massachusetts

1966 March–May. Amon Carter Museum of Western Art, Fort Worth, Texas

1966 May–July. Museum of Fine Arts, Houston, Texas

1966 September–October. University Art Museum, Albuquerque, New Mexico

# Selected Bibliography

EVER SINCE her earliest exhibitions, both O'Keeffe and her work have been magnets for an emotional and largely uninformative literature of vast dimensions, far too extensive to list fully in this catalogue. For this reason, the references below have been selected to include informative references of factual value, whether they are found in books, magazines, exhibition catalogues, or newspapers. A fair sampling of the wilder writings has also been included, because it is part of the picture, and so it belongs. Finally, it is always the paintings which speak most truly for O'Keeffe, not the word.

Since exhibitions of new work took place almost yearly from 1923 through 1946, files of the art press (magazines and newspapers) should be consulted for additional critical material which is of interest.     D.B.

STATEMENTS BY GEORGIA O'KEEFFE (includes writings, interviews, quotations)

An American Place, New York. Georgia O'Keeffe: Catalogue of the 14th Annual Exhibition of Paintings with Some Recent O'Keeffe Letters. 1937–38, Eight letters written to Alfred Stieglitz from Ghost Ranch, New Mexico.

——. Georgia O'Keeffe: Exhibition of Oils and Pastels. 1939. "About Myself."

——. Georgia O'Keeffe: Exhibition of Oils and Pastels. 1940.

——. Georgia O'Keeffe: Paintings – 1943. 1944. "About Painting Desert Bones." (reprinted in *Magazine of Art*, February, 1944.)

The Anderson Galleries, New York. Alfred Stieglitz Presents One Hundred Pictures. Oils, Watercolors, Pastels, Drawings, by Georgia O'Keeffe, American. 1923.

——. Alfred Stieglitz Presents Fifty-one Recent Pictures. Oils, Watercolors, Pastels, Drawings, by Georgia O'Keeffe, American. 1924.

Baur, John I. H. *Nature in Abstraction*. New York, 1958.

Kuh, Katharine. *The Artist's Voice: Talks with Seventeen Artists*. New York, 1962.

*MSS*. "Can a Photograph Have the Significance of Art: Statement." New York, December, 1922.

*New York Times*. Letter to the Art Editor. February 23, 1941.

*New York Times*. "Stieglitz: His Pictures Collected Him." December 11, 1949.

Nordness, Lee, ed. *Art: USA: Now*. New York, 1963.

BOOKS AND EXHIBITION CATALOGUES

An American Place. New York. Exhibition catalogues, 1930–1946, many with statements of interest.

Barr, Alfred H., Jr. *Masters of Modern Art*. New York, 1954.

Baur, John I. H., ed. *New Art in America: Fifty Painters of the 20th Century*. pp. 108–111, "Georgia O'Keeffe," by James Thrall Soby. New York, 1957.

Bry, Doris. *Alfred Stieglitz: Photographer*. Boston, 1965.

Bulliet, Clarence Joseph. *Apples and Madonnas*. Chicago, 1927.

Cahill, Holger, and Barr, Alfred H., Jr. *Art in America in Modern Times*. New York, 1934.

Cheney, Sheldon. *A Primer of Modern Art*. New York, 1924.

Coates, Robert M. *Profiles from the New Yorker*. New York, 1938.

Craven, Thomas. *Modern Art*. New York, 1934.

Eliot, Alexander. *Three Hundred Years of American Painters*. New York, 1957.

Frank, Waldo. *Time Exposures*. New York, 1926.

Frank, Waldo, and Lewis Mumford, Dorothy Norman, Paul Rosenfeld, Harold Rugg, eds. *America and Alfred Stieglitz, a Collective Portrait*. New York, 1934.

Friedman, Martin L. *The Precisionist View in American Art*. Minneapolis, 1960.

Geldzahler, Henry. *American Painting in the Twentieth Century*. New York, 1965.

Goodrich, Lloyd. *Pioneers of Modern Art in America. The Decade of the Armory Show, 1910–1920*. New York, 1963.

——. *Three Centuries of American Art*. New York, 1966.

Goossen, E. C. *The Art of the Real: USA 1948–1968*. New York, 1968.

Haftman, Werner. *Painting in the Twentieth Century*. New York, 1965.

Hapgood, Hutchins. *A Victorian in the Modern World*. New York, 1930.

Hartley, Marsden. *Adventures in the Arts*. New York, 1921.

*History of an American. Alfred Stieglitz:"291" and After*. Introd. by Henry Clifford and Carl Zigrosser. Philadelphia Museum of Art, 1944.

Hunter, Sam. *American Modernism: The First Wave. Painting from 1903 to 1933*. The Rose Art Museum, Brandeis University, Waltham, Massachusetts, 1963.

The Intimate Gallery. New York. Exhibition catalogues, 1925–1929, many with statements of interest.

Janis, Sidney. *Abstract and Surrealist Art in America*. New York, 1944.

Katz, Leo, and Webster, James Carson. *Understanding Modern Art*. New York, 1936.

Kootz, Samuel M. *Modern American Painters*. New York, 1930.

Lane, James W. *Masters in Modern Art*. Boston, 1936.

Mellquist, Jerome. *The Emergence of an American Art*. New York, 1942.

Metropolitan Museum of Art, New York. *100 American Painters of the 20th Century*. Introd. by Robert Beverly Hale. New York, 1950.

Mumford, Lewis. *The Brown Decades*. New York, 1931.

Museum of Modern Art, New York. *Paintings by Nineteen Living Americans*. 1930. [See also Museum's exhibition catalogues over the years.]

Northrop, F. S. C. *The Meeting of East and West*. New York, 1947.

[O'Keeffe, Georgia.] *The Work of Georgia O'Keeffe. A Portfolio of Twelve Paintings*. Introd. by James W. Lane and an appreciation by Leo Katz. New York, 1937.

[O'Keeffe, Georgia.] Georgia O'Keeffe Drawings. Introd. by Lloyd Goodrich. [Ltd. edition of ten drawing reproductions signed and numbered by the artist.] New York, 1968.

Phillips, Duncan. *A Collection in the Making*. New York, 1926.

Rich, Daniel Catton. *Georgia O'Keeffe*. The Art Institute of Chicago, 1943.

——. *Georgia O'Keeffe. Forty Years of Her Art*. Worcester Art Museum, Worcester, Massachusetts, 1960.

Rosenfeld, Paul. *Port of New York*. New York, 1924.

Rugg, Harold. *Culture and Education in America*. New York, 1931.

Rose, Barbara. *American Art Since 1900: A Critical History*. New York, 1967.

——. *American Painting: The Twentieth Century*. Cleveland, 1970.

Seligmann, Herbert J. *Alfred Stieglitz Talking*. New Haven, 1966.

Soby, James Thrall and Miller, Dorothy C. *Romantic Painting in America*. New York, 1943.

Wilder, Mitchell, ed. *Georgia O'Keeffe. An Exhibition of the Work of the Artist from 1915 to 1966*. Amon Carter Museum of Western Art, Fort Worth, Texas, 1966.

Whitney Museum of American Art. *Pioneers of Modern Art in America*. 1946. [See also Museum's exhibition catalogues over the years.]

### ARTICLES AND REVIEWS

"The Art of Georgia O'Keeffe." *Amerika*, [August, 1949?]

"Austere Stripper." *Time*, May 27, 1946.

Berman, B. Vladimir. "She Painted the Lily and got $25,000 and Fame for Doing It." *New York Evening Graphic Magazine Section*, May 12, 1928.

Bry, Doris. "Georgia O'Keeffe." *J. Am. Assoc. of Univ. Women*, January, 1952.

Crowninshield, Frank. "A Series of American Artists – in color: No. 1. Georgia O'Keeffe." *Vanity Fair*, April, 1932.

Duncan, Charles. " '291' Exhibitions: 1914–16. Georgia O'Keeffe, C. Duncan, René Lafferty." *Camera Work*, No. 48, October, 1916.

Fisher, William Murrell. "The Georgia O'Keeffe Drawings and Paintings at '291'." *Camera Work*, No. 49–50, June, 1917.

Flint, Ralph. "Lily Lady Goes West." *Town and Country*, January, 1943.

——. "Exhibitions in New York." *Art News*, Jan. 24, 1931; Jan. 2, 1932; Jan. 14, 1933.

"Fisk University Dedicates Alfred Stieglitz Collection." *The Crisis*, March, 1950.

Getlein, Frank. "In the Light of Georgia O'Keeffe." *New Republic*, November 7, 1960.

Genauer, Emily. "Art and Artists: Have You Ever Been All Blue?". *New York Herald Tribune*, April 16, 1961. [See also writings in *New York World Telegram, New York Post*.]

Goossen, E. C. "O'Keeffe." *Vogue*, March 1, 1967.

"Georgia O'Keeffe Turns Dead Bones to Live Art." *Life*, February 14, 1938.

"Georgia O'Keeffe, Who 'Makes Death Beautiful.'" *Art Digest*, March 1, 1937.

Gibbs, Jo. "The Modern Honors First Woman – O'Keeffe." *Art Digest*, June 1, 1946.

Hollis, Janette. "Two American Women in Art – O'Keeffe and Cassatt." *The Delphian Quarterly*, April, 1945.

Hunter, Vernon. "A Note on Georgia O'Keeffe." *Contemporary Arts of the South and Southwest*, November–December, 1932.

Kalonyme, Louis. "Georgia O'Keeffe: A Woman in Painting." *Creative Art*, January, 1928. (See also his articles in *Arts and Decoration* in 1926, 1927, 1933.)

Lawrence, Ruth. *Five Painters*. University Gallery, Minnesota University, 1937.

Luhan, Mabel Dodge. "Georgia O'Keeffe in Taos." *Creative Art*, June, 1931.

Kramer, Hilton. "The American Precisionists." *Arts*, March, 1961.

McBride, Henry. "Modern Art." *The Dial*, May, 1926. (See also McBride's writings in the *Sun, Creative Art, Art News*, and the art press over the years.)

McCausland, Elizabeth. "Georgia O'Keeffe." *Parnassus*, March, 1940. (See also McCausland writings in *The Springfield Daily Republican*.)

"Metropolitan Buys 3 Works in City Art Show." *New York Herald Tribune*, March 26, 1934.

Milliken, William M. "White Flower by Georgia O'Keeffe." *The Bulletin of The Cleveland Museum of Art*, April, 1937.

Mumford, Lewis. "O'Keeffe and Matisse." *New Republic*, March 2, 1927. (See also Mumford writings in the *New Yorker*, "The Art Galleries" 1933–36.)

*The Metropolitan Museum of Art Bulletin*. "A Report on American Art." January, 1950.

"Many Ways." *Time*, November 14, 1949.

Oaks, Gladys. "Radical Writer and Woman Artist Clash on Propaganda and its Uses." *The World*, March 16, 1930.

O'Brien, Frances. "Americans We Like: Georgia O'Keeffe." *The Nation*, Oct. 12, 1927.

O'Doherty, Brian. "Art: O'Keeffe Exhibition." *New York Times*, April 11, 1961.

"O'Keeffe's Woman Feeling." *Newsweek*, May 27, 1946.

"O'Keeffe's Pineapple." *The Art Digest*, February 15, 1940.

"The Paintings of Georgia O'Keeffe in Taos." *Atelier*, June, 1931.

Pemberton, Murdock. "The Art Galleries." *New Yorker*, February 20, 1926. (See also his writings in this column 1926–32.)

"Pineapple for Papaya." *Time*, February 12, 1940.

Plagens, Peter. "A Georgia O'Keeffe Retrospective in Texas." *Artforum*, May, 1966.

Pollitzer, Anita. "That's Georgia." *The Saturday Review of Literature*, November 4, 1950.

Read, Helen Appleton. "The Feminine Viewpoint in Contemporary Art." *Vogue*, June 15, 1928.

"Retired American Art." *Newsweek*, July 5, 1948.

Rich, Daniel Catton. "The New O'Keeffes." *Magazine of Art*, March, 1944.

———. "The Stieglitz Collection." *Bulletin*, The Art Institute of Chicago, Nov. 15, 1949.

Rosenfeld, Paul. "American Painting." *The Dial*, December, 1921.

———. "The Paintings of Georgia O'Keeffe." *Vanity Fair*, October, 1922.

Sabine, Lillian. "Record Price for a Living Artist." *Sunday Eagle Magazine* (Brooklyn, N. Y.), May 27, 1928.

Seiberling, Dorothy. "Horizons of a Pioneer." *Life*, March 1, 1968.

Seldis, Henry. "Georgia O'Keeffe: At 78. Tough-Minded Romantic." *Los Angeles Times West Magazine*, January 22, 1967.

Seligmann, Herbert J. "Georgia O'Keeffe, American." *MSS* (New York), March, 1923.

Soby, James Thrall. "To the Ladies." *The Saturday Review of Literature*, July 6, 1946.

"Stieglitz Assails W.P.A. Art as 'Wall Smears.'" *New York Herald Tribune*, Dec. 3, 1946.

Strand, Paul. "Georgia O'Keeffe." *Playboy*, July, 1924.

Tyrrell, Henry. "New York Art Exhibitions and Gallery News." *The Christian Science Monitor*, June 2, 1916.

———. "Esoteric Art at '291'." *The Christian Science Monitor*, May 4, 1917.

Wilson, Edmund. "Stieglitz Exhibition [Seven Americans] at the Anderson Galleries." *New Republic*, March 18, 1925.

Willard, Charlotte. "Georgia O'Keeffe." *Art in America*, October, 1963.

"Wonderful Emptiness." *Time*, October 24, 1960.

C.Z. [Zigrosser, Carl.] "An American Collection." *The Philadelphia Museum Bulletin*, May, 1945.

# Whitney Museum of American Art

The black-and-white plates were made and printed in duotone offset by The Meriden Gravure Company, Meriden, Connecticut. The color engravings were made by Publicity Engravers, Inc., Baltimore, Maryland, and were printed at the Press of A. Colish, Mount Vernon, New York. The type was composed by The Stinehour Press, Lunenburg, Vermont. The text was printed by The Meriden Gravure Company. The production of the catalogue was coordinated by Doris Bry.

The black-and-white illustrations were made from photographs supplied by Miss O'Keeffe and by the lenders. Twenty-five of these were made by Robert Mates and Paul Katz, fourteen by Charles Uht, and two by Geoffrey Clements. The color plates were made from transparencies by Malcolm Varon.